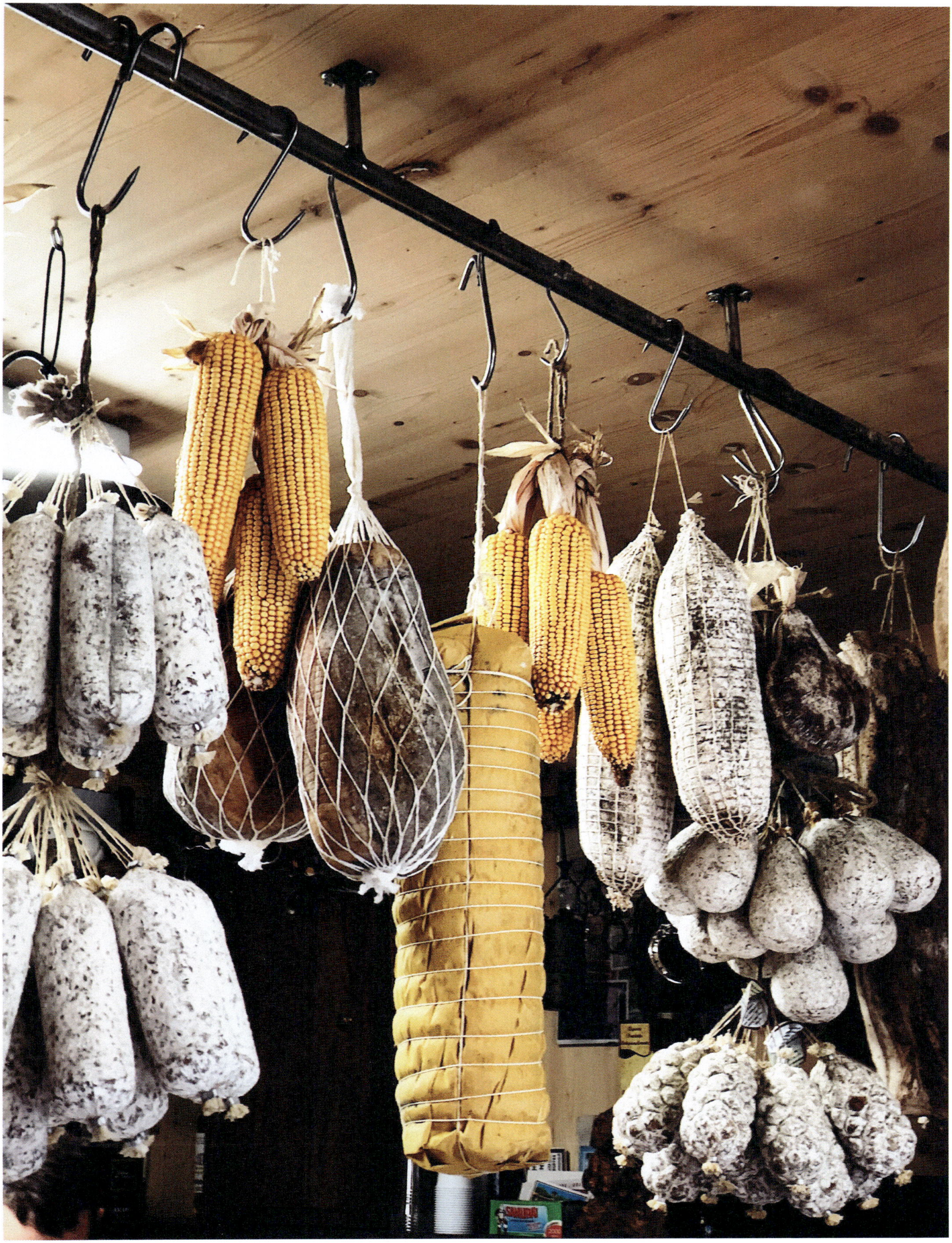

WELCOME

Ciao,

benvenuti in Umbria, welcome to Umbria. The central region of Italy, the land of fairytales, religious fervor, and nourishing food. A land to live slowly, letting nature, flavors, legends, ancient celebrations, and wine inebriate you.

This Simposio will guide you through some - slow traveling means having to choose, but a second issue will come - of Umbria's towns. You will explore Perugia, Gubbio, Orvieto, Spoleto, Montefalco, Norcia, and Scheggino. Of each, you will take home a story, a personage, a sentiment, or an experience. Of all, you will discover the flavors of their traditional cuisine and the beauty of their alleys.

Set your mind to the fairytale mood. As always, we will cross the line of reality. We will enjoy the foggy dimension of maybe and the fun state of why not. Italy's heritage is made of this: ancient beliefs, uncertain origins, the merging of cultures, and breathtaking results.

Get ready to feast over chestnuts and beans, chicken and duck, peasant's cuisine and truffles, sausages, and seasonal vegetables.

Get ready to sip wine wrapped in a mantel, facing a bonfire, waiting to see angels pass, or witches, or griffons.

Get ready to witness Etruria merging into Middle Ages, the sixties avant-garde into modern jazz, and religious fever into everyday life.

Get ready for Umbria!

Claudia

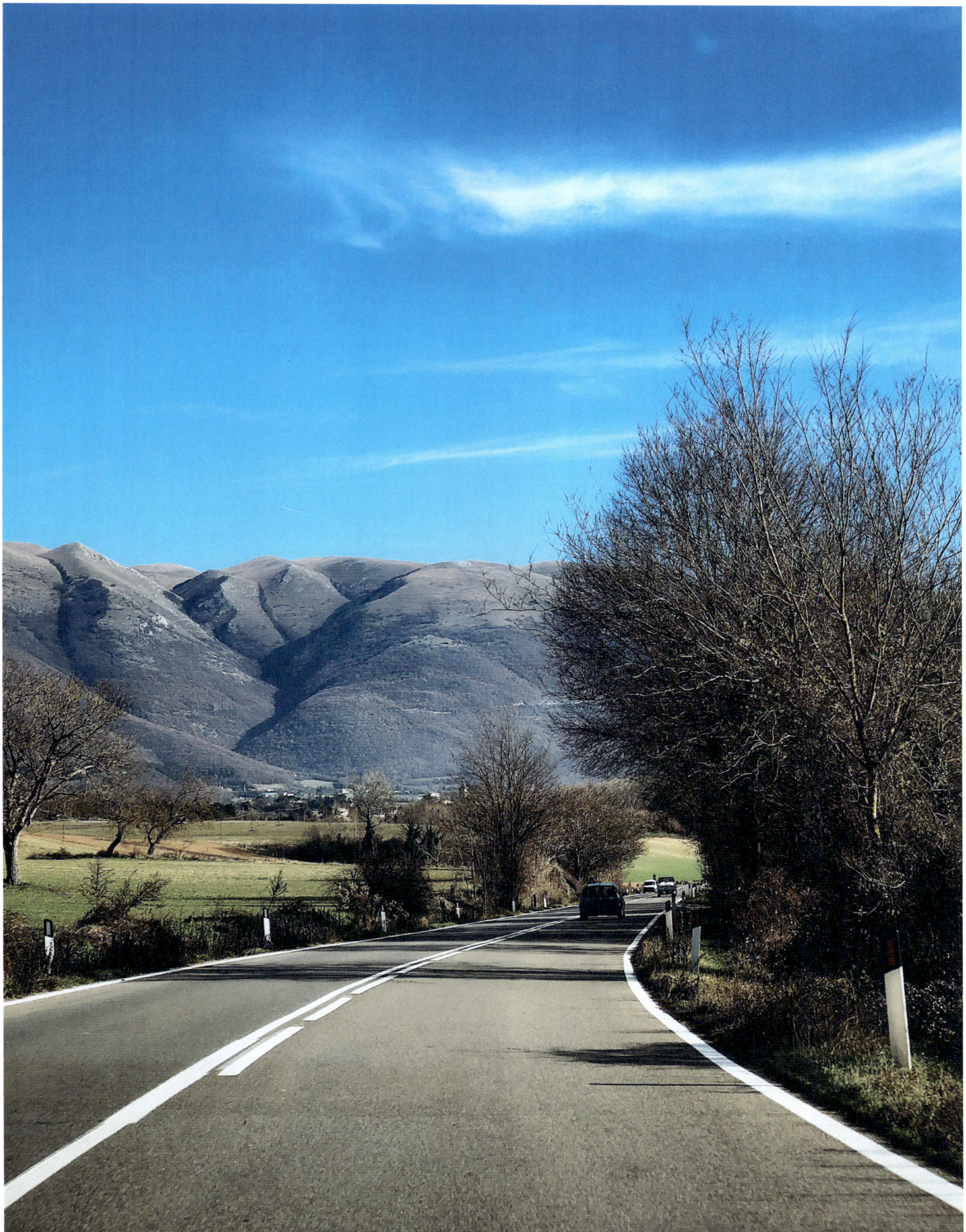

COOKING NOTES

Recipes are in grams, ounces, and cups whenever possible. Servings are primarily for two, but you can double the recipe if desired. The majority are fall recipes, but some are for you to cook and celebrate other seasons.

Remember to read the recipes all the way. It helps a lot. First, you are conscious of the ingredients and the tools that you will need; second, you will behave intentionally, knowing, in broad terms, what's coming next.

I also recommend gathering all the ingredients in your workstation before starting to cook. I try to indicate peeling, chopping and dicing at the best time, but you can prep them before to make things easier.

Restock your pantry with lentils, farro, cornflower, semolina, and 00 flour. Don't forget a bottle of good quality extra virgin olive oil. Cold-pressed would be marvelous. As always, when cooking Italian, aromatic herbs are fundamental: parsley, marjoram, rosemary, and sage. May I suggest you buy tiny plants and keep them in your garden/balcony/window? Spices have their special role, too: dry fennel flowers (or seeds) and juniper. Nuts will bring autumn flavors and hues: almonds and hazelnuts. Most of the ingredients are easily gatherable, and I try to give you substitutes whenever I consider it feasible with decent results.

I've seen Prosciutto, pancetta, Pecorino, tomato paste (Passata, not sauce), and canned tomatoes (Pelati) in many supermarkets abroad.

You might need to search a bit for truffles. Amaretti cookies might not be common, but you can try Italian delicatessens or online. You can substitute fresh baker's yeast with the dry version; the proportion is 3:1 - divide the fresh grams/ounces per three.

Finally, use good quality wine for cooking, it goes in your body just like the one you drink, and it does change the flavor of your food! Sagrantino Passito will be the protagonist of a delicious gnocchi dish. You may substitute it, but it is also worth a little searching around. It is a vine unique to Umbria and perfect as a dessert wine too.

Finally, find yourself a great butcher: we will rediscover duck and chicken liver, which, please, believe me, is delicious when appropriately cooked!

tartufi norcinerie prodotti del parco

BRANCALEONE DA NORCIA

OFFERTISSIMA
5 SALAMI € 20,00
1 SUINO
1 CERVO
1 COGLIONI DI MULO
1 SALAME AL CINGHIALE
1 CACCIATORINO
6 PEZZI € 30,00
1 SALAME CINGHIALE E TARTUFO
1 SALAME NURSINO
1 COGLIONE DI MULO
1 SALSA TARTUFATA DA 100g
1 METRO DI SIENA
1 CACCIATORINO
5 PEZZI € 25,0
1 GUANCIALE/PEPE/PEP
1 SALAME ALLA BIRRA
1 PICCANTISSIMO DELL'UMB
1 PECORINO DI FOSSA
500g STRANGOZZI DELL'UMB

INDEX

TRAVEL
08 Bucket List
10 Umbria
14 Eating In Umbria
30 Perugia
30 The Griffon
34 Luisa Spagnoli
38 Pinturicchio
48 Gubbio
48 If I Were Little Red Riding Hood
50 Festa Dei Ceri
60 Orvieto
60 A Winter In Orvieto
72 Spoleto
72 If I Were A Hippie
82 Montefalco
82 A Year Of Celebrations
86 Umbria Wines
94 Norcia
94 Religion, Today
108 Scheggino
108 Viva Le Donne

CULTURE
116 CHRISTMAS
120 Stelle Di Natale

RECIPES
16 Crescia Bread
18 Chestnut and Chickpeas Soup
20 Chicken And Rabbit Fricco
22 Pollo Alla Cacciatora
24 Porchetta Duck
26 Raisin Pancotto
28 Biscotti Della Trebbia
42 Farro Alla Perugina
44 Gobbi Alla Perugina
46 Torello Alla Perugina
54 Patè All'Eugubina
56 Acquacotta Di Gubbio
58 Imbrecciata Soup
66 Lumachelle Orvietane
68 Pizza Gialla
70 Torta Di Orvieto
76 Strangozzi
78 Strangozzi Alla Spoletina
80 Crescionda Di Spoleto
90 Gnocchi Al Sagratino Passito
92 Tozzetti
94 Attorta
102 Marjoram Oil
104 Spaghetti Alla Norcina
106 Lenticchie In Bianco
108 Lu Pizzallocu
114 Lumachine Alla Schegginese
116 Uovo Lento Al Tartufo
124 Boiled Chestnuts
126 Grape Juice Overnight Oatmeal
128 Nonna Clara's Mackerel Pasta
130 Broccoli Cream And Grilled Swordfish Pasta

7

BUCKET LIST

GOOGLE THE IMAGES OF: "Vite Maritata". It is how Umbrians used to grow vines in the past - since the Etrurian era. "Maritata" means married. The vines were let to wildly climb up poplars, maples, elms, and olive trees in a non-damaging but loving embrace. Very romantic.

LISTEN TO: Anything by Luigi Mancinelli, the composer from Orvieto. Light a scented candle, pour yourself some tea, and enjoy every note!

READ: The Decamerone's novel about Andreuccio Da Perugia, his Sicilian "sister", and his adventures in Naples.

SHOP: the Orogami jewels in Orvieto - https://www.orogami.com. Check their BUBBLES collection and the beautiful silver and enamel rings!

PINTEREST: all the paintings by Pinturicchio, Renaissance painter from Perugia, and uncommon personage.

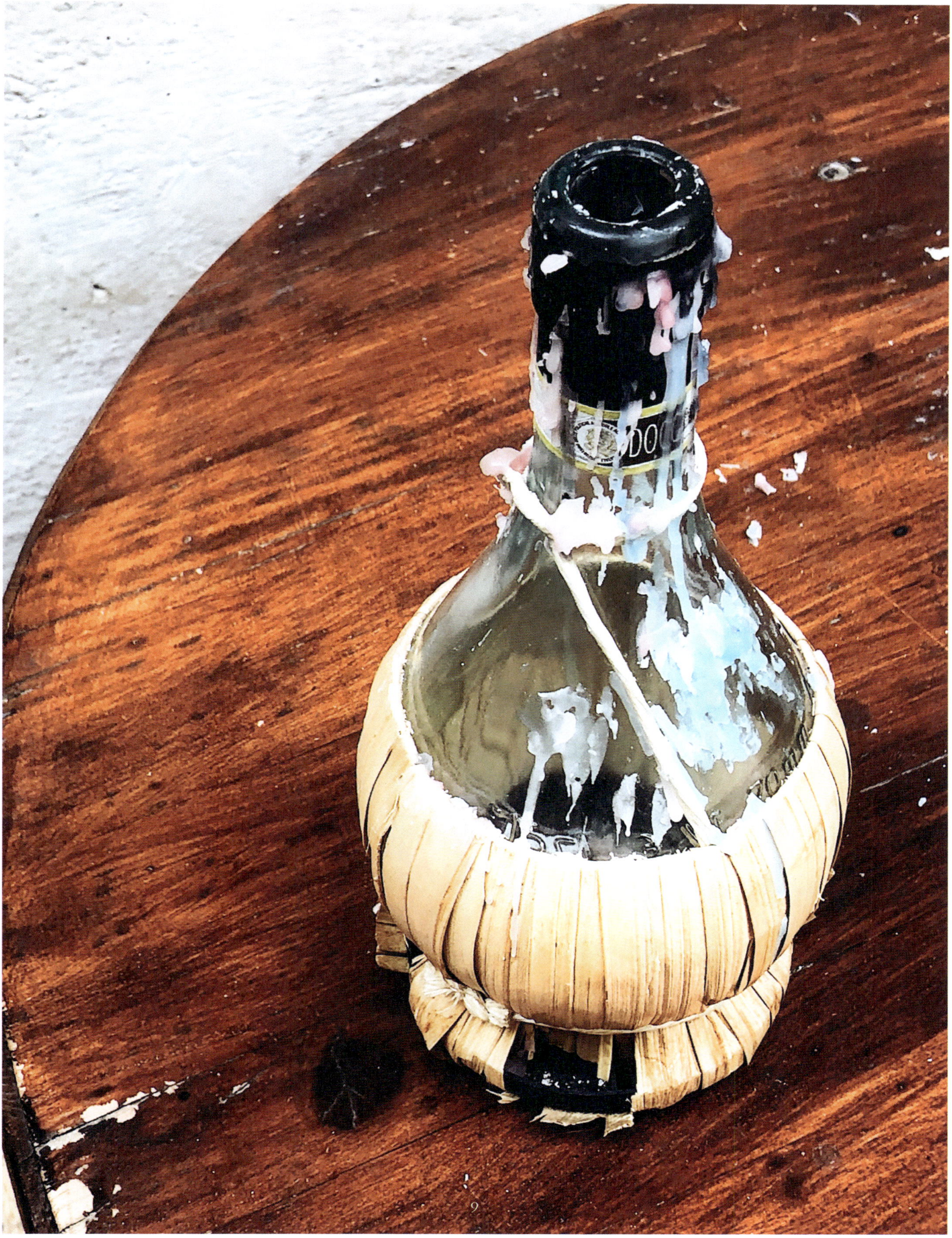

UMBRIA

We came back from our last Umbria road trip with the car exploding. We had, as always, gone a bit too far with wine, oil, and local specialties shopping. But when you have your own car, and dozens of excuses like "wholesale prices", or "I can't find it in Rome", or even "let's sustain the local economy", the sky is not the limit anymore. You forget you could order online or through an email. You neglect your promise to diet once home. You only want to bring a piece of that wild nature back with you. You want to eat like the people smiling at you while pouring you yet another drop of wine. You want your toasted bread to taste just like the one they offer you copiously surmounted by olive oil. You want to use spices and herbs sapiently, like the cook you friended at the restaurant where it took you only a couple of days to become a habitué. You want all the dark green of the forests to sprout in your heart. You want to devour your meals voraciously while a cold wind swirls around the rocky room. Not even a menace anymore, just the perfect setting for your truffled eggs. And the duck ragu. And the cookies tossed in the fortified, sleep-aiding wine.

Umbria is a region to visit during the fall or during the winter. Because it's pure comfort.

Visiting Umbria is like watching a medieval movie. Would you like to see the knights under a shining sun? No, you want a foggy forest. Would you enjoy seeing people bathing and sunbathing? No, you want them next to a bonfire, cooking game meat, drinking red wine. To me, at least now that I'm writing, Umbria is the dreamland of late autumn and winter. The rocky fortresses, the gothic churches, the enormous Prosciutti hanging from the ceiling. The wicker baskets loaded with truffles or Porcini mushrooms. Even the way people talk, like chanting. Perfect for tales recounted sitting next to the chimney. Umbrian pleasures require cold, windy days., short days, so the lights must be lit soon. Candle lights, if possible.

Umbria is known as the green heart of Italy. It is positioned perfectly at the center of the peninsula. And the territory is intensely dark green. Forest green. It is landlocked and plentiful of rivers. I have no doubt the majority of the fairytales happened here.

The towns are small and relatively close one to the other. You can sleep in one place and from there reach practically any destination on your list. We stayed in the tiny Torgiano and are planning to go back soon.

You need a car to explore the region, to hop from a city to a perched town, from a valley

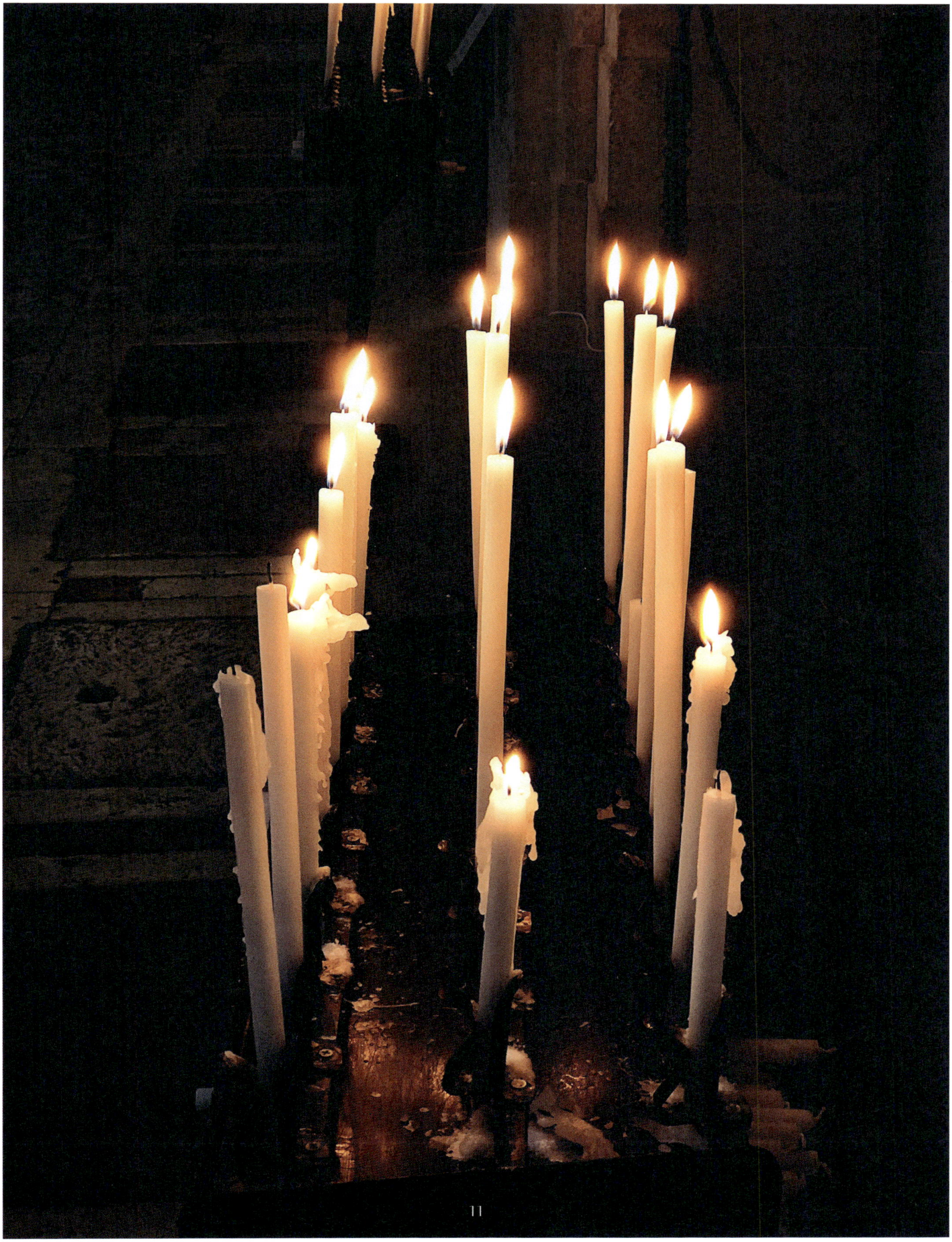

to a hill. Like a faun. So that you can decide where to stop for a more comprehensive visit, a meditative stop, or lunch. Walking shoes are mandatory for the slopes, the many, many slopes.

Etruscan and Umbri (indigen populations) left behind the grand tradition of winemaking, later influenced by the Roman Empire and the papal subjugation. And more recently by tentatives of globalization and the blessed rebellious rediscovery of ancient, unique to the territory vines.

Umbria is a mystic region. Italian Catholicism - and where there is Catholicism, there is paganism, at least here in Italy - has colonized the roots, the culture, and the folklore since the mid-1500s. Popes have dominated, ruled, drank, eaten, and lived in Umbria. Folklore has married religion, and much of it has forged the region's identity. Many saints were born and raised here, and at least a few have gained notable positions in shaping the nation, politics - until 1948, Christianity was the state religion -, and arts. San Benedetto, San Francesco, Santa Chiara, Jacopone da Todi... The late Middle Ages and Renaissance were fertile ground to the foundation of monasteries and dogmas, to the rise of the Papal State, and, consequently, to rich commissions for religious art.

The fact that this art was both religious fervor and propagandistic instruments didn't seem to matter much.

Great families, politicians, philosophers, and artists themselves were often portrayed as Madonnas, saints, and devotees. Painters and sculptors competed to represent spiritual magnificence. They enclosed messages, personal beliefs, and intimate secrets of their patrons.

Since the early 1900s, patrons have returned. The Festival Dei Due Mondi has transformed Spoleto into a city stage for great names and debutants. The Umbria Jazz Festival, both in Summer and Winter, has given a charismatic identity to both Perugia and Orvieto. Again, for acclaimed stars and unknown newbies. More magic, depth, and devoutness have enriched a land that impregnates everything with otherworldliness: stories, traditions, art, and food.

Let's experience some of it.

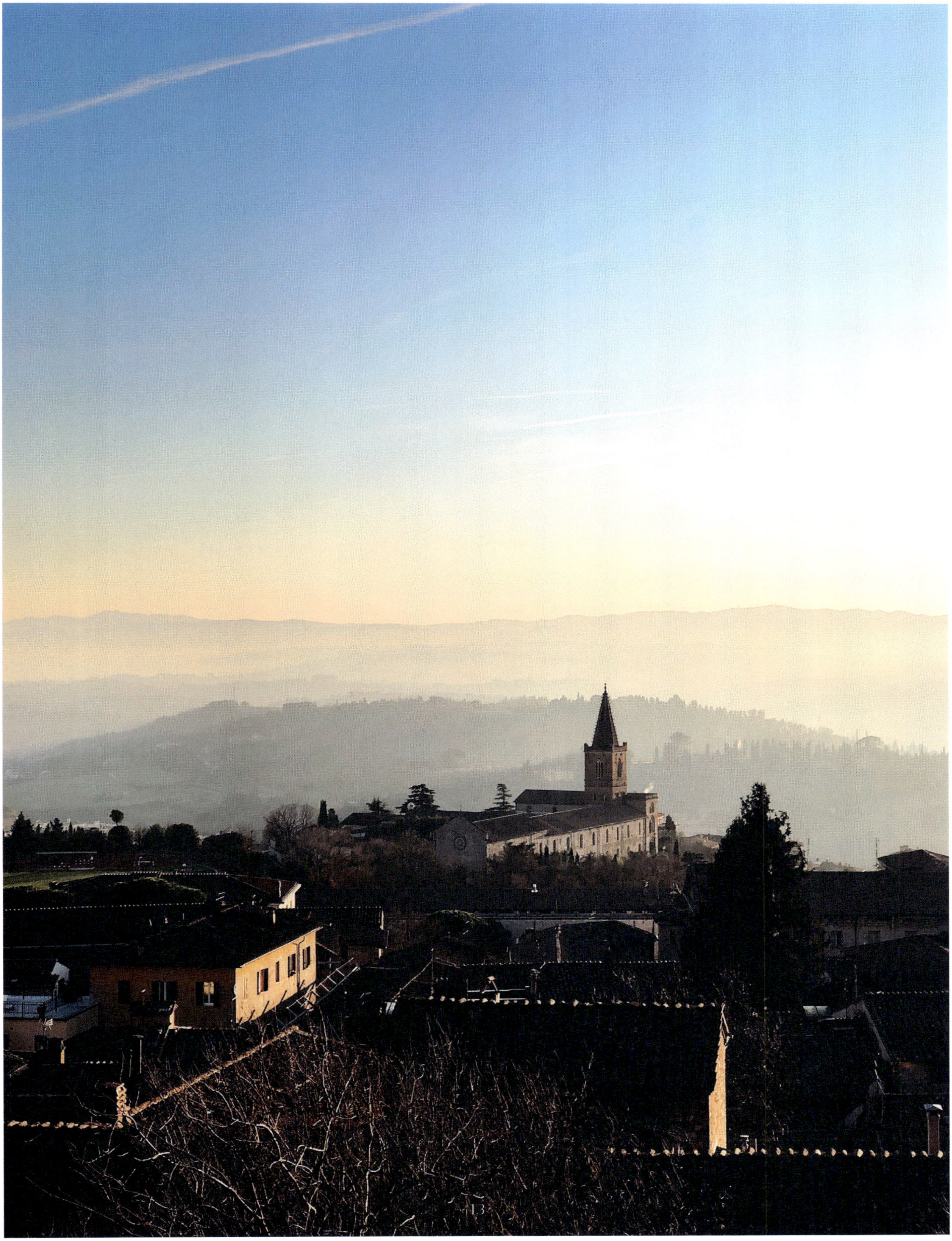

EATING IN UMBRIA

Tell an Italian you're going to Umbria, and his expression will change. Salivation will increase, eyes will sparkle, and you might even perceive an embarrassing rumbling from the belly.

Eating in Umbria is festive. When you sit at a restaurant, you feel like you're sitting at a Christmas table in a household. At least a few dishes between pork, hare, rabbit, goose, duck, squab, wild game, and chicken will appear on the menu. Slow roasted with herbs and spices, the food is accompanied by chestnuts, polenta, mushrooms, and copiously dusted with truffle flakes. Sometimes raw, many times briefly sauteed in olive oil.

"Grani", a word used to indicate both beans and legumes, equally share the stage: lentils, beans, and farro will delight your palate.

The bread is unsalted, sharing the custom with bordering Tuscany. Then, covered with unfiltered, pungent Umbrian olive oil.

And the wine? The wine is reason enough for millions of people from all over the world to drive or fly here. To dedicate days to tasting, savoring, and purchasing Sagrantino, Orvieto DOC, and Trebbiano Spoletino.

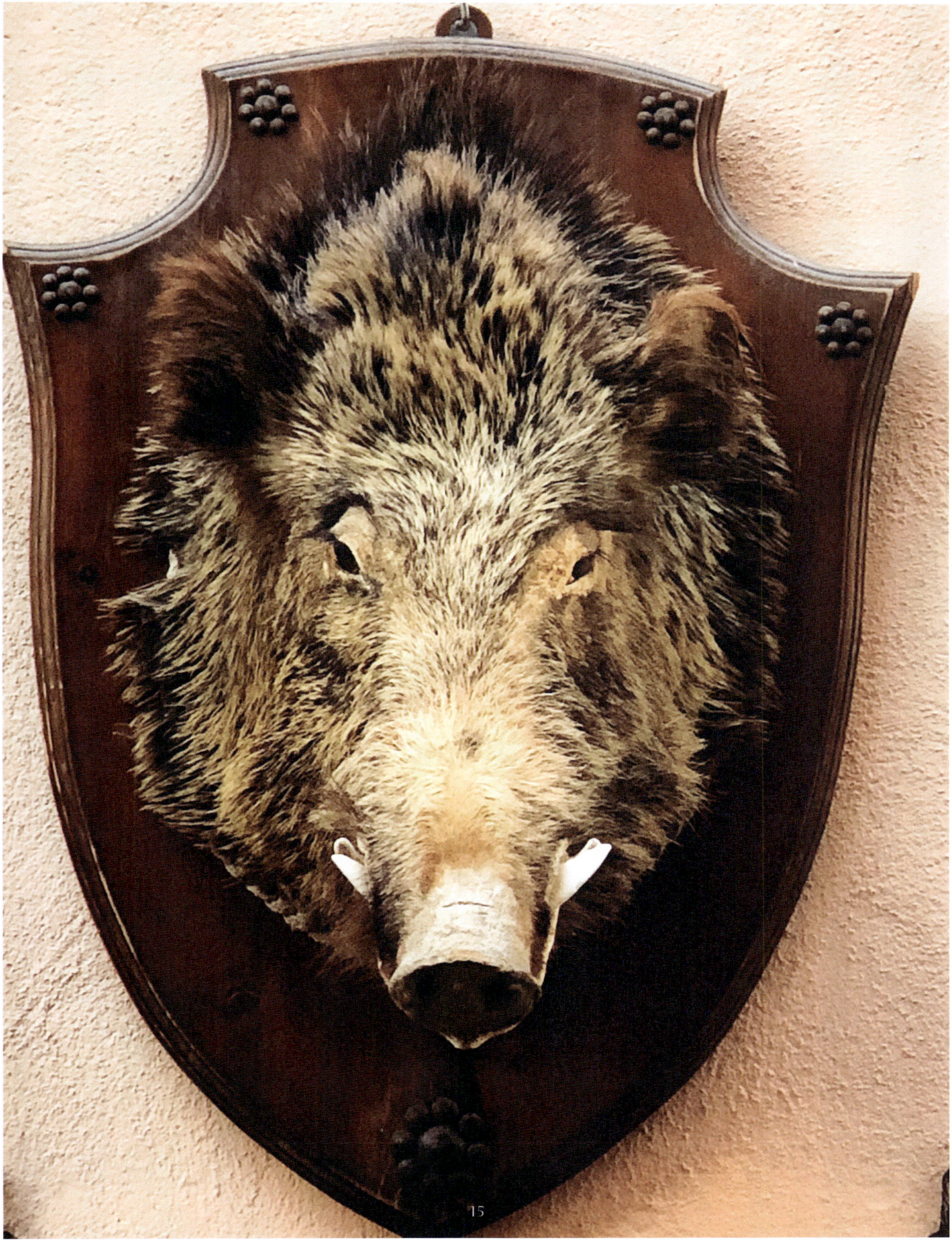

CRESCIA

Crescia is a round flatbread cooked in the ancient times under the ashes of the household fire on traditional cast iron skillets called Testo. The reason why it is also called Torta (cake) Al Testo.
With slight variations, it is cooked everywhere in Umbria. But the ancient recipe features only flour, water, salt, and a rising agent, most often baking soda.
Pair it with any of the juicy meat recipes coming next to collect every drop of condiment with a joyous Scarpetta!

Ingredients for two flatbreads:
250 gr (8.8 oz or 1 + 3/4 cups + 2 tablespoons + 1 teaspoon) of 0 flour
20 gr (0.7 oz or 1 + 1/2 tablespoon) of extra virgin olive oil
1/2 teaspoon of baking soda
125 gr (4.4 oz or 1/2 cup + 1 tablespoon) of sparkling water
1/2 teaspoon of salt
a cast-iron skillet

Place the flour in a bowl or the mixer's bowl.
Add the olive oil, baking soda, and water and work until fully amalgamated (dough hook on). Add the salt and work until you get a smooth and elastic dough - you might need to add a tablespoon of water or two.
Cover the dough and place it in a warm spot of your house for three hours.
Heat the skillet until, by dusting it with a pinch of flour, it goldens. Divide the dough into two equal pieces and work each with your hands to get a rounded shape about two and a half centimeters/one inch thick.
When the skillet is hot, transfer the first disc, pierce the base with a fork, and cook for about three minutes - pay attention not to burn the bottom. Flip it on the other side and cook for two to three minutes. Repeat for the other disc.
That's it, serve your Crescia hot or wrap it in a cloth until the next day. If it hardens too much, wrap it in aluminum foil and place it in a preheated oven at 150°C/300°F for about ten minutes.

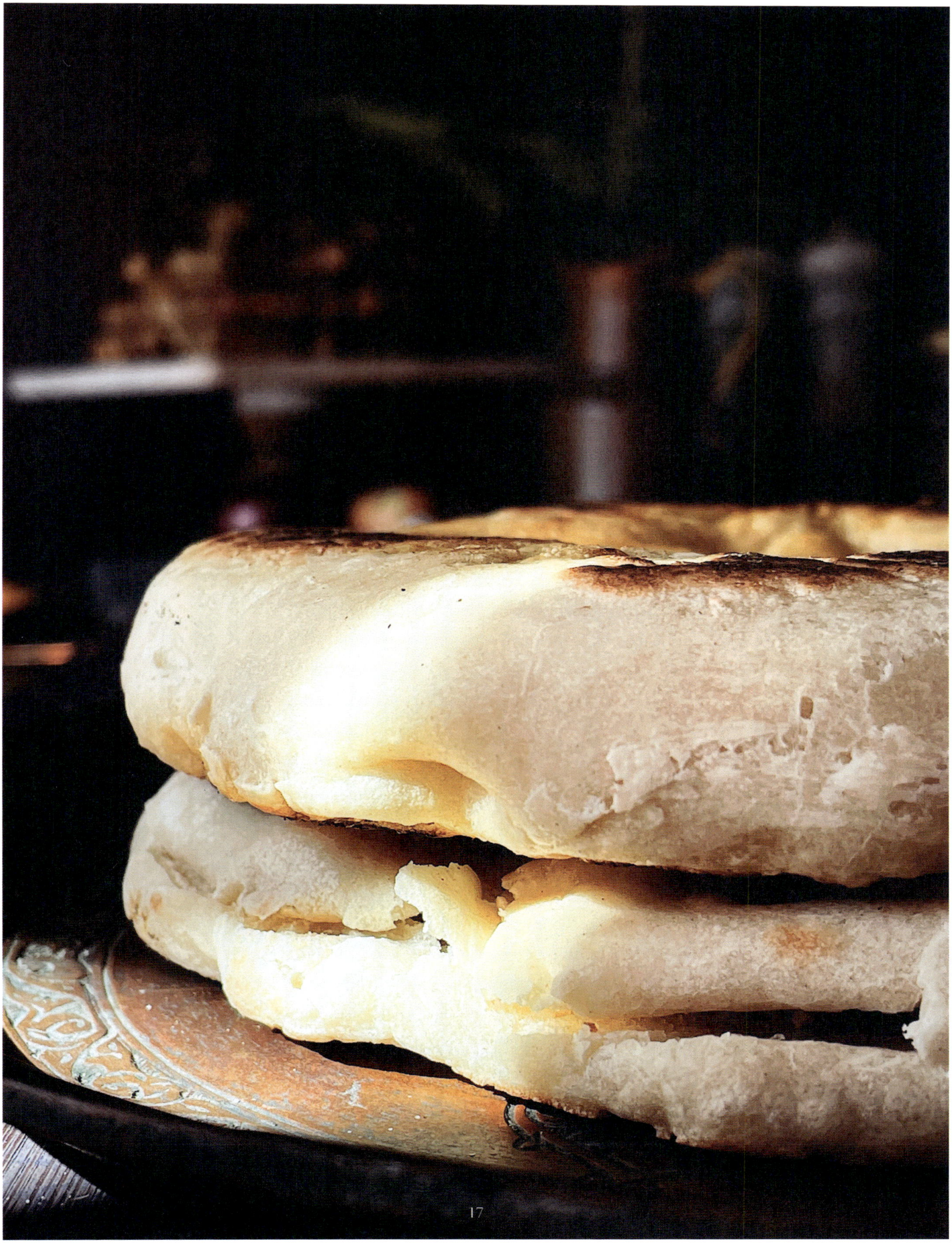

ZUPPA DI CECI E CASTAGNE

The chickpea and chestnut soup is a traditional Umbrian recipe for the fishless Christmas Eve feast. But I would devour a bowl at least once a week while chestnuts are in season. The flavors' contrast is perfect, texture too.

Ingredients for two:
120 gr (4.2 oz) of dried chickpeas - or about 240 gr (8.5 oz) of precooked
100 gr (3.5 oz) of roasted chestnuts
1/2 garlic clove
1 tablespoon of chopped fresh parsley
2 tablespoons of extra virgin olive oil
50 gr (1.8 oz or a little less than 4 tablespoons) of tomato paste (Passata)
salt
black pepper
4 slices of rustic Italian bread

If dry, soak the chickpeas overnight. Drain them, transfer them to a pot, cover them with water, and cook them, covered and over low heat, for two hours.
Drain them, but keep the cooking water.
Preheat the oven to 180°C/350°F.
Carve an X-shaped cut on the round side of each chestnut and transfer them to a baking rack or a baking sheet - one layer. Roast them for twenty-five to thirty minutes.
With the help of a kitchen cloth, peel them while still hot. You can wait five to ten minutes to let the temperature decrease a bit.
Peel and finely chop the garlic and finely chop parsley.
In a medium pot, heat the olive oil for a minute or so and add the garlic and parsley trite. Sauté for about five minutes on medium heat - don't burn the garlic!
Add the chestnuts, mix and sauté five minutes more.
Add the tomato paste, stir and cook for a couple of minutes. Add the drained chickpeas, cover with water by two inches and add a pinch of salt. Mix, cover, and cook, on the lowest heat, for an hour. Taste for salt and add a few grinds of pepper, as per your taste.
When ready, toast the bread slices, place them on the bottom of the serving bowls and pour the soup over.
Serve your soup hot and devour it!
You may also sprinkle some grated parmesan cheese on top.

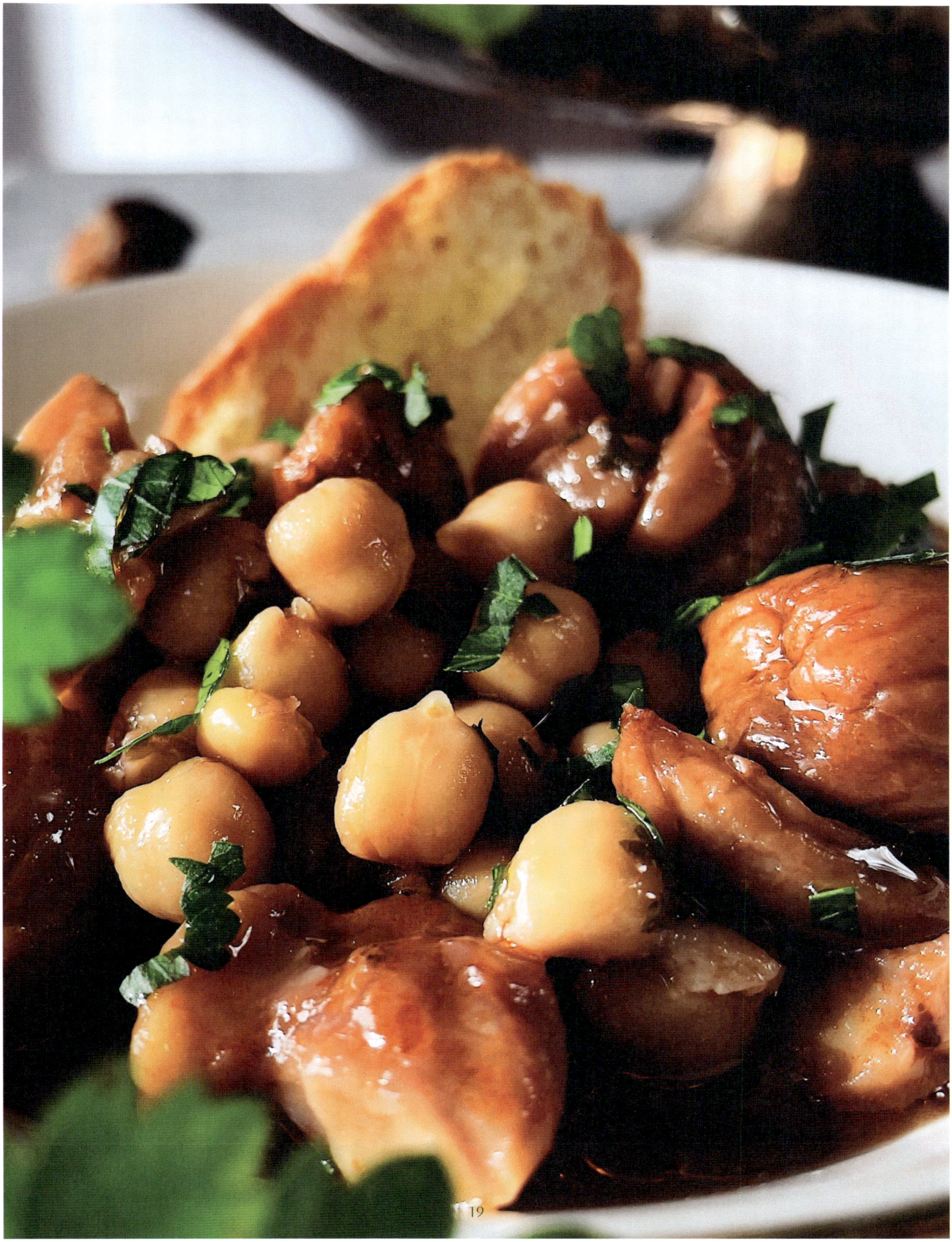

FRICCÒ

There are many recipes for Friccò, fundamentally a full-of-herbs and wine style to cook white meats. In Umbria, you'll find chicken, rabbit, duck, and lamb recipes. Sometimes with tomatoes, sometimes with onions. I chose to make this one, with chicken and - optionally - rabbit, "in bianco" (white) as an alternative to Pollo Alla Cacciatora "in rosso" (red, with tomatoes). Enjoy your Friccò as tradition prescribes: served with a Crescia.

Ingredients for two:
about 300 gr (10.5 oz) of chicken breast and/or rabbit saddle
50 gr (1.8 oz or about 3 slices) of Prosciutto Crudo
1 garlic clove
1 bay leaf
2 sage leaves
1 small rosemary sprig
1/4 cup of white wine
1 tablespoon of black olives - pitted
1 tablespoon of extra virgin olive oil
salt
black pepper

Cut the chicken and rabbit meat into medium pieces.
Crush the garlic clove with the blade of a large knife - no need to peel it.
Julienne the Prosciutto Crudo.
Heat the olive oil in a medium pan, add the meat, and seal all sides over medium heat for a little more than five minutes. Toss in the garlic clove, the bay leaf, sage, and rosemary. Sprinkle the meat with a few pinches of salt, mix and cook, over medium/low heat for about ten minutes, stirring every now and then.
Pour in the wine, mix, and let it evaporate, rising to medium heat for about five minutes.
Add the Prosciutto, cover, and cook ten minutes more over medium heat.
Make sure the meat is well cooked and taste it for salt.
Add the olives, a few grinds of pepper (two to five), mix and sautè for five minutes.
Serve your Friccò hot!

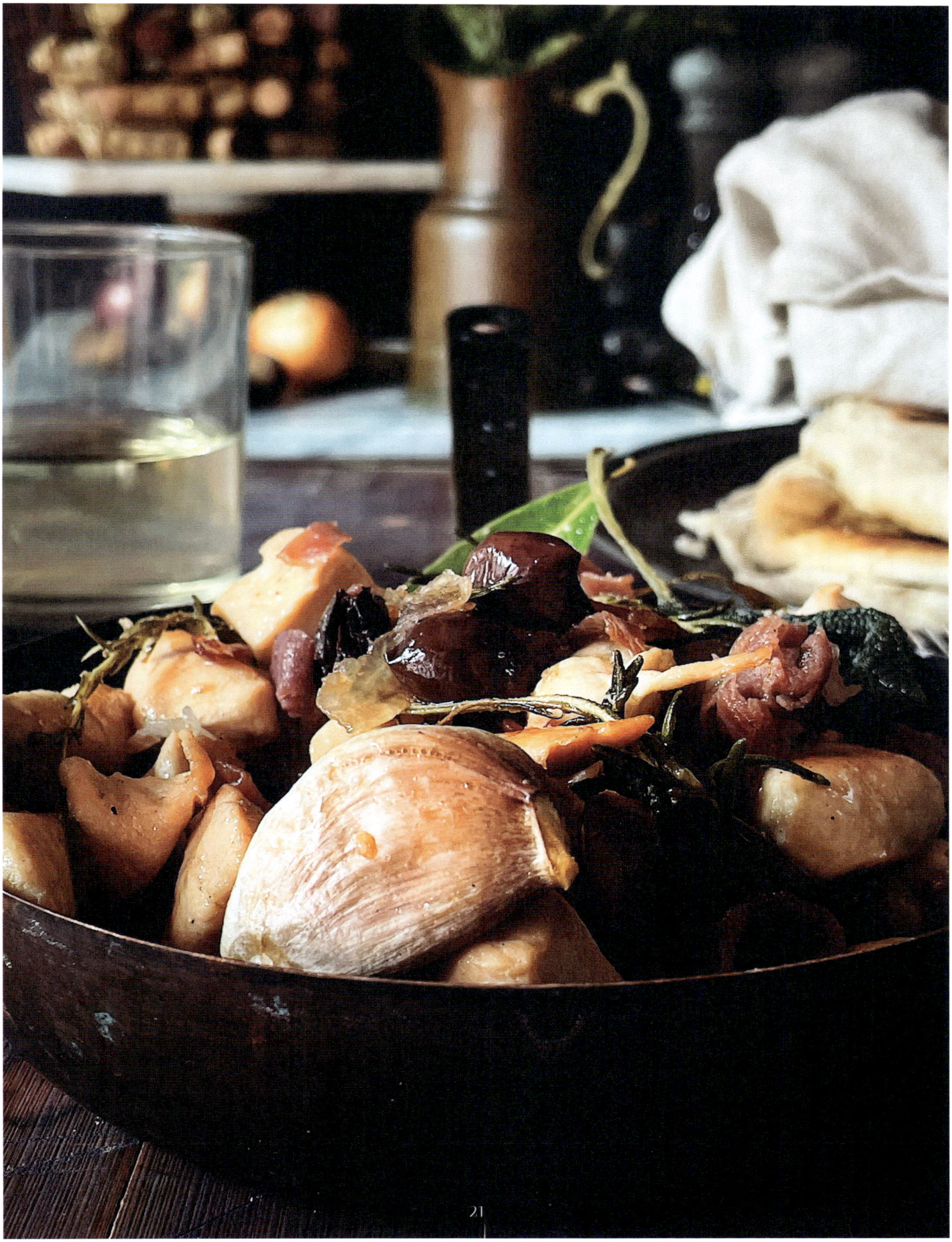

POLLO ALLA CACCIATORA

Pollo Alla Cacciatora is a recipe common to many, if not all, Italian regions but with local peculiarities.
It is called Alla Cacciatora, the hunter way, because the meat - not solely chicken - is flavored with the herbs hunters could find on their way back home.
Here's how they make it in Umbria. Rosemary and sage flavor the chicken, and the tomato sauce gives moisture and sweet peaks of flavor. As always, recipes vary from city to city, family to family, and kitchen to kitchen!

Ingredients for two:
2 chicken thighs - or about 300 gr/10.5 oz of chicken in pieces
1 tablespoon of extra virgin olive oil
1 garlic clove
1/2 rosemary sprig
3-4 sage leaves
1/4 cup of dry white wine
250 gr (8.8 oz) of tomato paste - Passata
salt
black pepper

Peel and crush the garlic clove with the blade of a large knife.
In a large skillet, heat the olive oil over medium heat, add the garlic, and brown it for about five minutes - don't burn it!
Meanwhile, finely chop the rosemary needles and the sage leaves.
Add them to the skillet and brown for a minute.
Add the chicken thighs or pieces and sear all sides for three to four minutes, until golden brown.
Pour in the wine and let the alcohol evaporate for a couple of minutes. The alcohol smell should be gone.
Sprinkle the meat with a pinch of salt and add a quarter cup of water to the skillet.
Cover and cook, on medium heat, for fifteen minutes.
Uncover, pour in the tomato paste, another pinch of salt, and a few grinds of pepper - about ten. Mix a bit, flip the meat on the other side - or stir - cover and cook thirty minutes more.
Your Hunter's Chicken is ready! Serve it hot with toasted bread or Crescia.

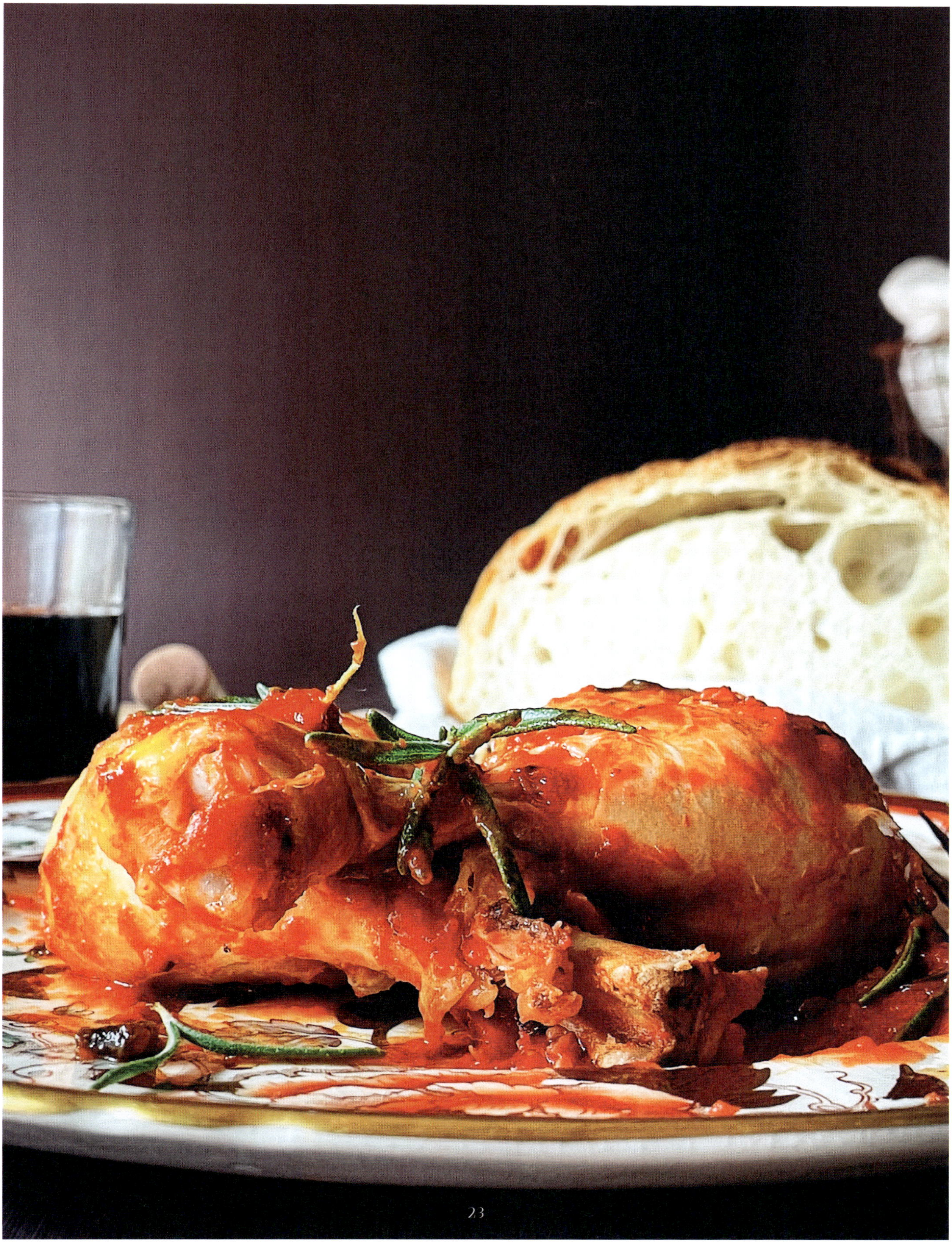

ANATRA IN PORCHETTA

This duck meat recipe is called "In Porchetta" because it is prepared with the same ingredients used - in many central regions - to make Porchetta: boneless pork stuffed with herbs and slowly roasted over wood for at least eight hours.
The recipe is for four servings because a duck breast weighs nearly one kilo. But I'm sure you'll be glad to have someone over for dinner or freeze the leftovers for another grand feast!

Ingredients for four:
1 kg (2 lbs) of duck breast
100 g (3.5 oz) of Prosciutto Crudo fat
2 rosemary sprigs
1 teaspoon of (dry) wild fennel flowers or seeds
3-4 sage leaves
2 tablespoons of red wine vinegar
1 pinch of sea salt
a few grinds of pepper - about 10
a Dutch oven or a similar large cooking pot

Separate the Prosciutto fat from the rest and use the leftovers to make two delicious paninis!
Trite together - you can use a grinder - the wild fennel flowers, salt, pepper, and Prosciutto fat. Add the vinegar and mix well.
Rub the whole surface of the duck with the mixture.
Place the duck inside the Dutch oven, cover it and let it marinate for at least two hours. Or overnight in the refrigerator.
Preheat the oven to 220°C/430°F.
Cover and cook the duck for forty to forty-five minutes (consider this timing for every kilo/two pounds of meat). But after thirty minutes, reduce the temperature to 180°C/350°F. After the total forty-five minutes, uncover the casserole and cook twenty minutes more to golden the surface and gain a soft crust.
Every now and then - let's say twice or thrice -, open the oven and use a spoon to collect the juices from the bottom and drizzle them over the meat.
Ready! Serve the duck hot, sliced, and covered in its cooking juices.

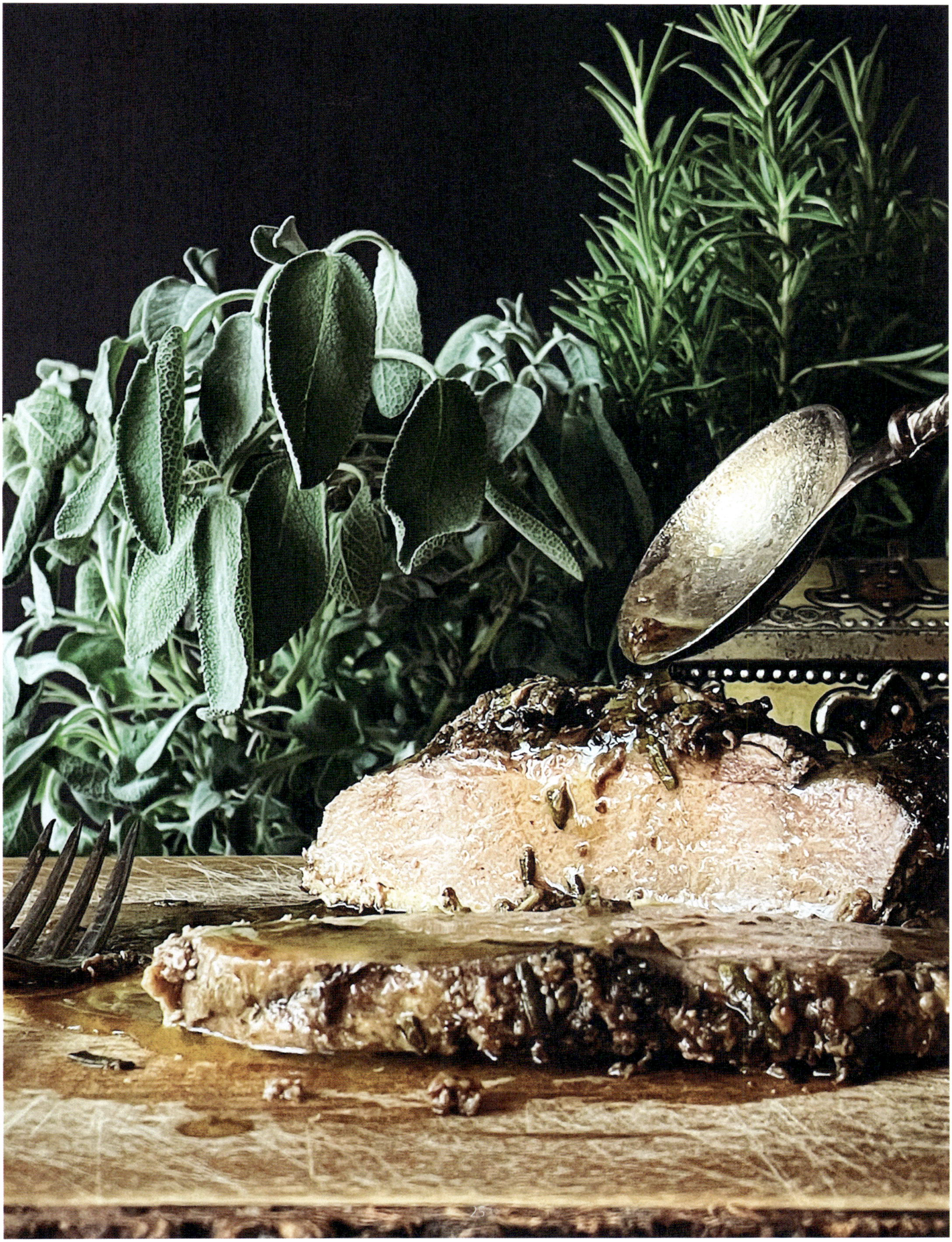

PANCOTTO CON UVETTA

Throwing away bread is a sin, any elder in Italy will tell you. Mindful of a time food was scarce.
After searching and experimenting with many traditional recipes from all over the peninsula that use stale bread, I can only agree. Also, because some dishes are pure primordial pleasure. Here's a sweetish recipe from an Umbria peasants' kitchen: cooked bread with raisins.

Ingredients for each serving:
1 slice of stale rustic Italian bread of about 30 gr / 1 oz
1 tablespoon of raisins
1 tablespoon of olive oil
salt
pepper

Dice the bread into medium pieces - with your hands or a knife.
Place the pieces in a small pot and add water to cover.
Cook, over the lowest heat on your stovetop, for fifteen minutes.
Add the raisins and half the olive oil, stir, and cook ten minutes more. You may need a tablespoon of water or two by the end of the cooking.
Turn off the heat, sprinkle with a pinch of salt and a few grinds of pepper.
Mix and serve hot. Lastly, sprinkle with the remaining olive oil.

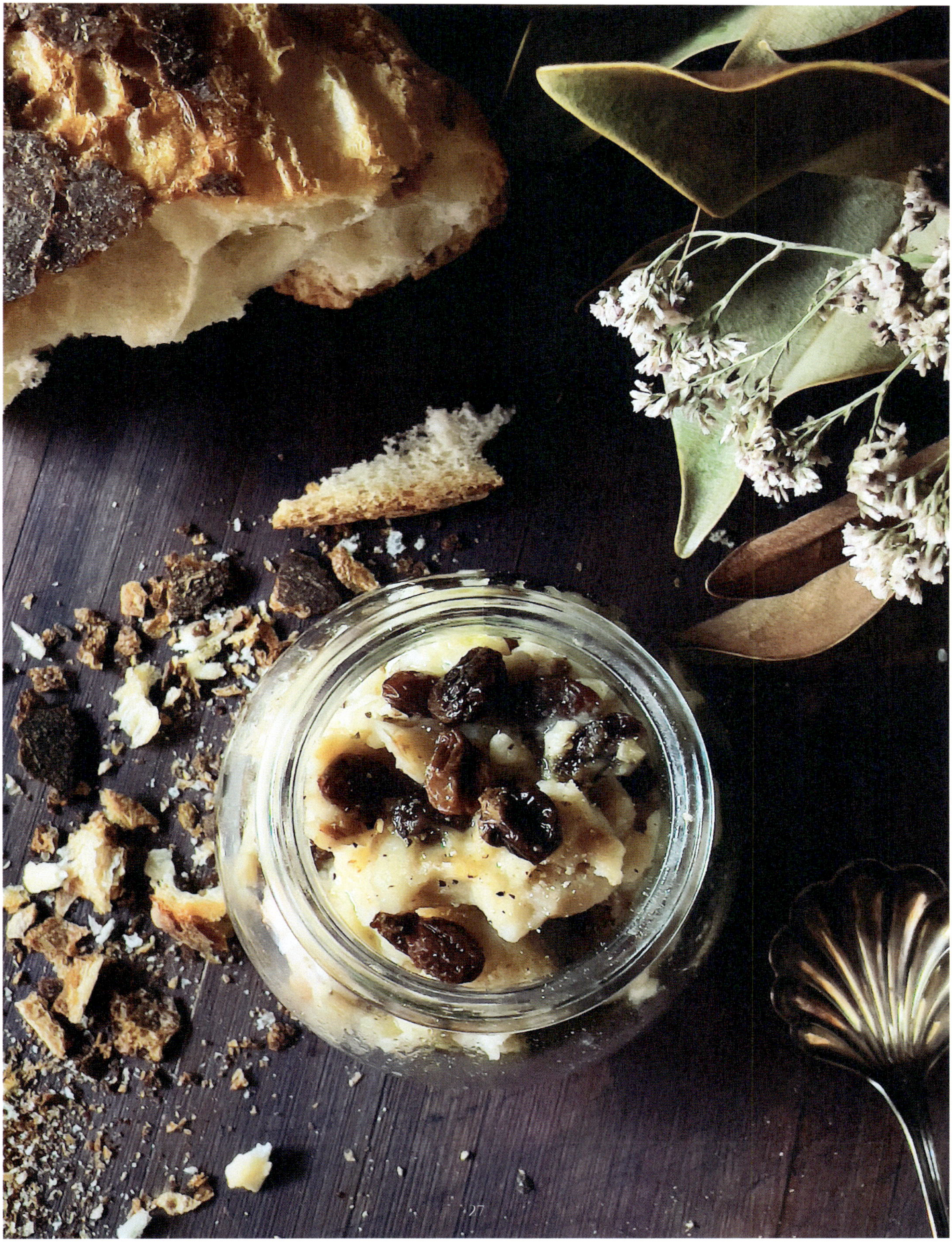

BISCOTTI DELLA TRESCA

Tresca is an Umbrian word for harvest. These cookies were baked and offered to the workers in the countryside during their hard-working days. Usually with a glass of wine to dip them in.
They are low in sugar and what we call Biscotti Da Inzuppo, dipping cookies. Not necessarily in wine, although delicious, but also in milk, for breakfast. Remember? Cookies in Italy are often eaten for breakfast.

Ingredients for 16-20 cookies:
240 gr (8.5 oz or 1 + 3/4 cup) of 00 flour
60 gr (2 oz or 1/4 cup + 2 tablespoons + 1 teaspoon) of brown sugar
50 ml (1.8 oz or 1/4 cup) of cow milk
2 eggs
the zest of 1/2 lemon
20 gr (0.7 oz or 2 tablespoons) of extra virgin olive oil
1 pinch of salt
2 teaspoons of baking powder

Preheat the oven to 180°C/350°F.
Place the sugar, milk, eggs, lemon zest, and olive oil in a mixing bowl. Add a pinch of salt and whisk to amalgamate.
Add the flour and the baking powder and mix well. Use the kneading hook of your mixer or a wooden spoon. You will get a sticky mixture.
Line an oven tray with parchment paper.
With the help of two tablespoons, collect a spoonful of dough at a time and transfer it to the oven sheet - not too distanced as the cookies will grow but mostly in height. Shape and flatten each ball with your hands as much as you can.
Bake the cookies for ten to fifteen minutes or until slightly golden.
Ready, serve them hot or at room temperature, or store them in a jar for up to a week.

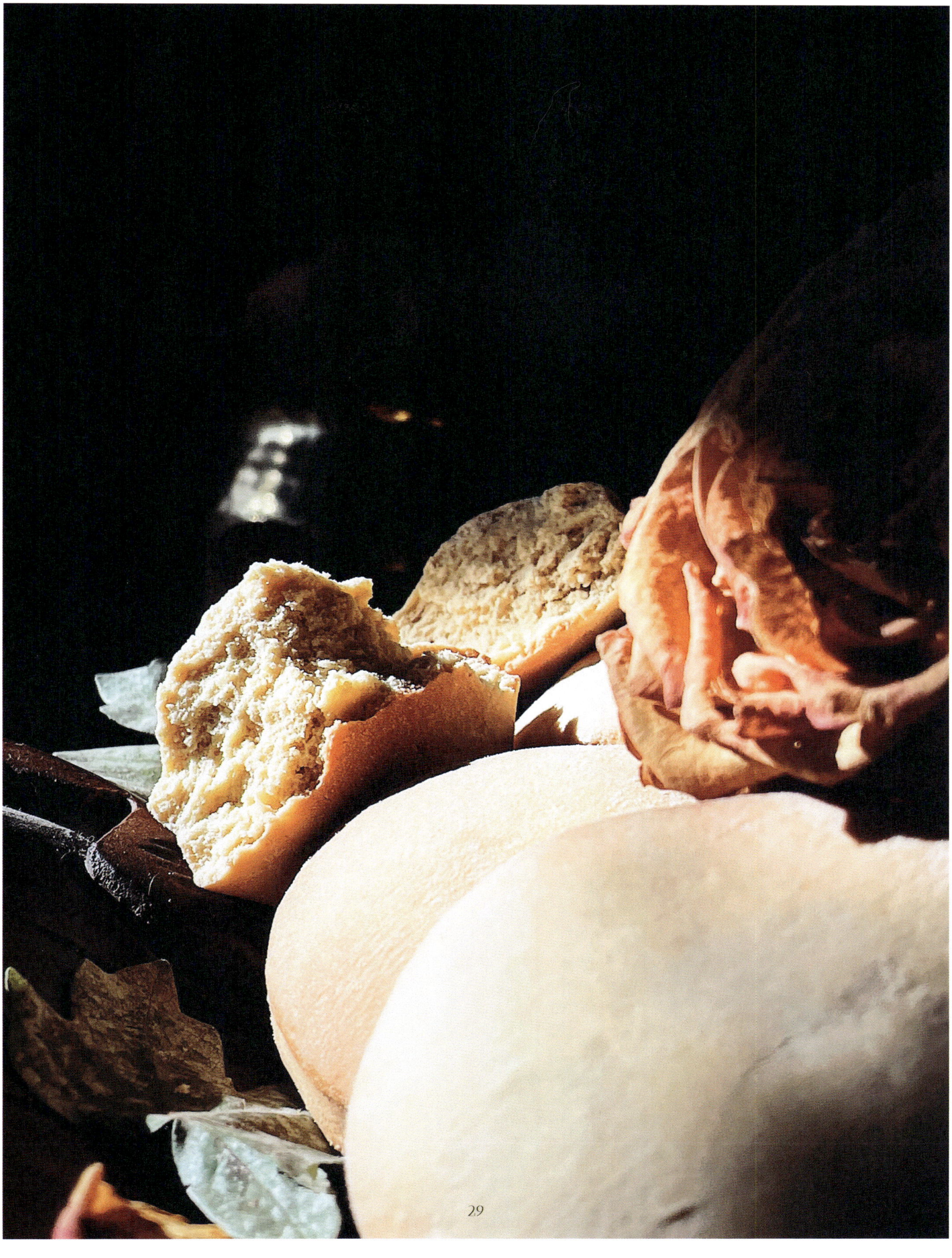

PERUGIA

Sometimes people don't realize the contradictions in their words or actions.
It happens to me much more often than I'd like to admit. So often in fact, that it makes me question my brain functions. It is like temporary blindness, like wearing blinders that block the vision of logical, unequivocal cues. Like being momentarily convinced that one and one make three.
Can we pause for a minute?
I want to give you a valid explanation: feelings. Troublesome feelings. Once it's rage, once is anxiety. Sometimes it's guilty feelings. Rarely happiness.
It may take a vast range of interval lengths to clarify your sight, contract the jaw, and blame yourself for your temporary rhapsody. It may take more time, sometimes infinity, to forgive yourself and pat your shoulder, smiling at your humanity.
But now I must ask Perugini one thing: how much more time do you need to realize the griffin is not your ally?
Grifoni, or Grifi - griffins - are mythological creatures. They are half lion - lower body - and half eagle – upper body. A hybrid of two regal creatures: the king of the lands and the king of the skies.
They are tough and bold like the lion and acute and smart as the eagle.
In the Middle Ages, someone advanced the theory that their claws were powerful revealers of poison. Changing color when in contact.
According to Greek mythology, griffins lived on the Rifei Mounts, the most northern region on earth – probably the Northern Pole. Apollo's hideout and the land of Hyperborean: healers and diviners. Griffins had the duty of guarding their gold. An occupation assigned because of their fierceness matched to intelligence.
In ancient, unspecified times, a griffin frolicked the countryside between Perugia and the near town of Narni. It had a preference for domestic animals that it would devour night after night. Cows and sheep disappeared in minutes. People were desperate. Desperate enough to suspend the rivalry between the two municipalities and organize a hunting mission.
Once captured and killed, Narni kept the beast's flayed body, while Perugia kept the skin. That's why the creature on Perugia's emblem is white, while the one on Narni's is red.

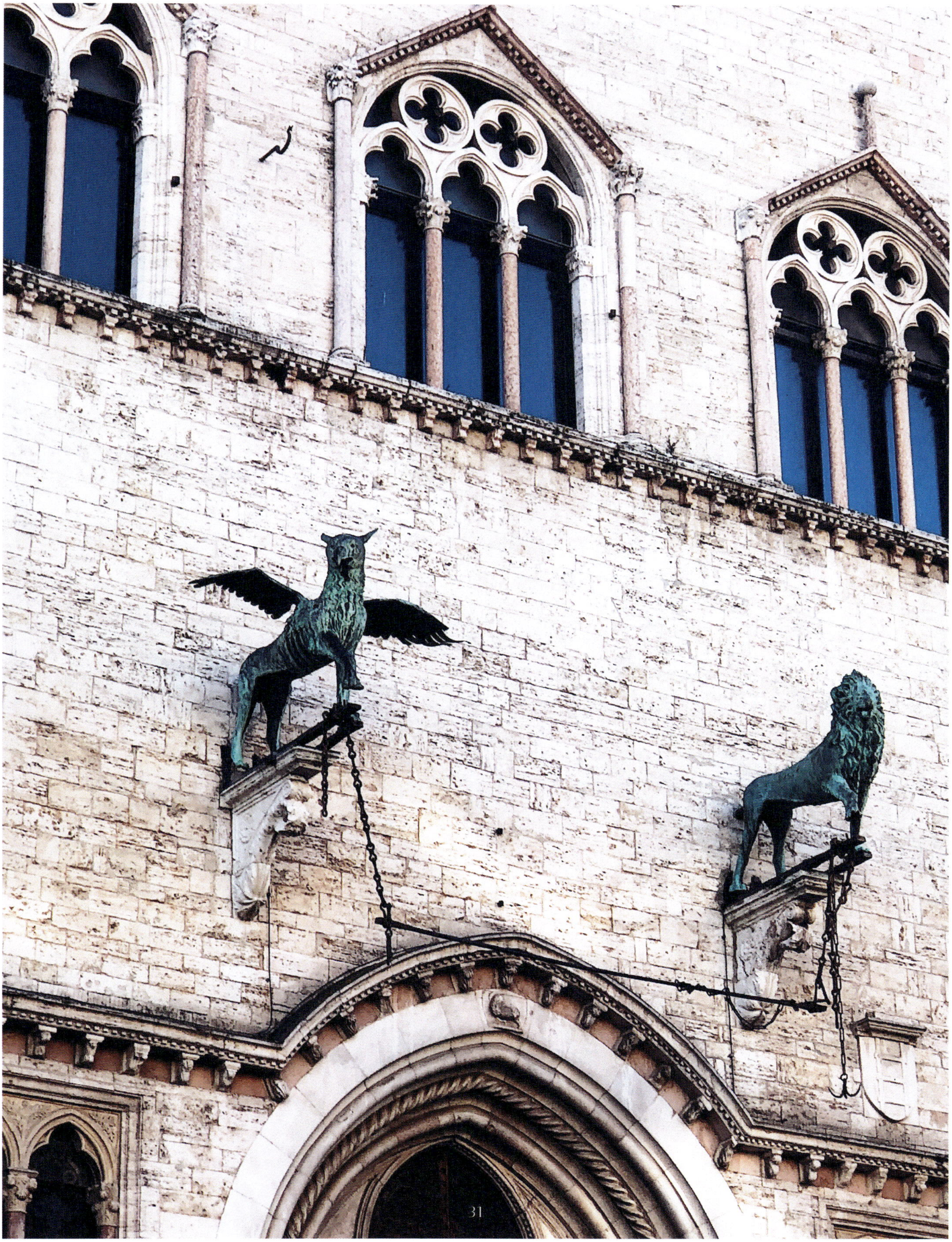

Ever since, Perugia's totem animal has been the griffin. It is supposed to protect the city with its strength and acute vision.

Maybe, once defeated, griffins grow fond of their executioners. But history has proven quite the opposite.

Perugini are closed and diffident. And this is not an exaggeration or a generalization. It is my experience and of millions of visitors. Each time I've toured the city, I've got angry at someone because of a face, snap, or rudeness. And left, exasperated, earlier than I had planned. You must be absolutely autonomous when you visit. Don't ask for favors, suggestions, or driving directions. Go, breathe in beauty and history, but have everything organized, even food. Ask for recommendations beforehand, and never, never, ask for the even slightest change in a procedure, a timetable, or a menu. Keep distance, and they'll let you in.

The explanation given is years and years of dominations and exploitation, especially under the Pontifical State.

Just as an example, although quite significant, in 1531, a new papal tax over salt was issued. The citizens, already in pecuniary, decided to not consume salt anymore. Still, nowadays, Umbrian bread is unsalted, just like in Tuscany. My husband hates it.

Eight years later, the tax was furtherly increased. Causing a furious protest. An excommunication from Pope Paolo III. And menaces of armed intervention.

Fury raised, and a popular assembly decided to put the city in the hands of Ridolfo Baglioni, the scion of one of the wealthiest families in Perugia, to move war against the pope.

All pumped, they spent days and months planning their victory and giggling at the impending defeat of the papal army.

But laughs - and the rampant scion - muted after a few skirmishes. The disparity of forces was ridiculous. They had to choose between decimation and a white flag. Ridolfo assumed the responsibility of the candid drape and negotiated: undisturbed entrance to the city but no more killing.

Not satisfied, the pope ordered the destruction of an entire neighborhood. Hundreds of houses, dozens of towers, a hospital, and a convent, all possessions of the Baglioni family, were razed to the ground, and the debris was destined to the building of a military structure: Rocca Paolina. Perugini were forced to work at the construction. Unpaid.

Really, my friends, I'd think twice, even thrice, of changing your totem animal. All I read in this story is sweet, delayed revenge!

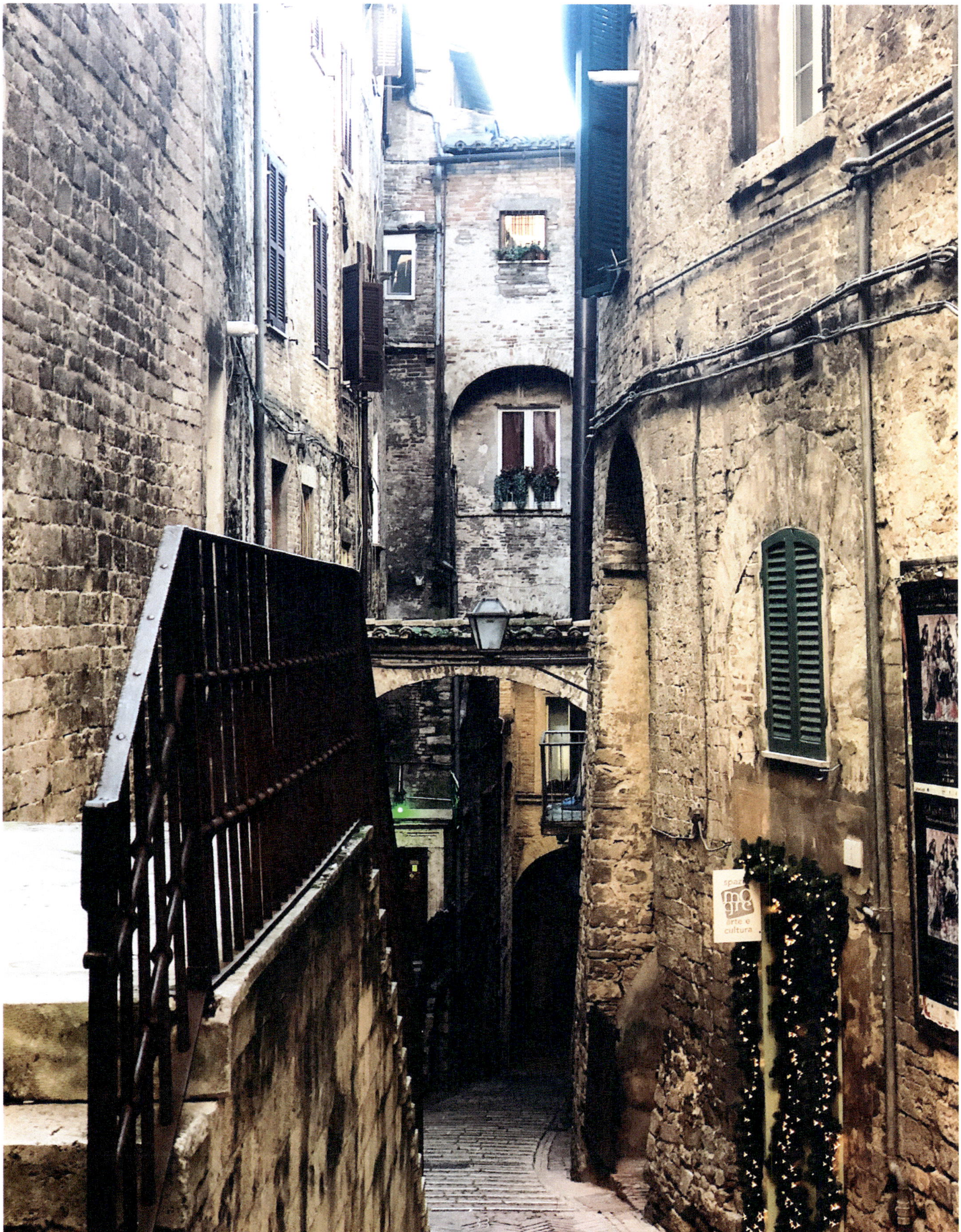
arte e
cultura

LUISA SPAGNOLI

"My nonna only dressed in Luisa Spagnoli" - it was a time when your wardrobe was made of only a few indestructible and timeless pieces. It is how my husband commented on the ending of my long babbling about yet another brilliant and successful Italian woman I had read about. All I could think instead was how perfect the moment would've been if we had two Baci Perugina to snack on.

Luisa Sargentini, born in Perugia on October 30, 1877, married Annibale Spagnoli in her early twenties. But she didn't appreciate the joys of householding as much as the ones of entrepreneurship. As her husband found when she convinced him to take over a drugstore, turn it into a confiserie, and lastly, expand through a partnership with some friends - one of them being Francesco Buitoni. She couldn't even vote - the company was founded in 1907, and women in Italy gained the right only in 1946 - but she knew how to boss. In the beginning, the business was florid. People loved to concede kids - and themselves - a chocolaty treat after the Sunday mass and bring more home, for the family or for friends. More employees were hired, more chocolate was produced, and more was distributed in the peninsula. Then WWI came, and men had to leave. Some came back; others didn't.

The first hurdle for the company was, of course, to survive. In order to survive, they needed to sell. To sell, they needed products. For products, they needed workers.

Women, left alone at home, didn't have the same money as before, but they had more time and little supervision. Luisa decided it was time to add a nursery to their factory: their new workers would've needed that and many breastfeeding permits. But the war hadn't taken away only the men, the money, and many commodities: it had wiped away the spirit. The mood was low and dark, darker than the chocolate left on the counters of the Perugina shops. Frivolities for other times. Innovation was the only way out. This is what Luisa was probably thinking, one night, desperately wandering around the labs. And waste was certainly not admittable anymore she must have grunted, eyeing the hazelnut grain: offcuts. In a matter of hours, the Cazzotto - Italian word for punch - was born: the rescued hazelnuts were incorporated into a gianduia paste, shaped into tiny one-bite bonbons, surmounted by a whole hazelnut, and covered with the "Luisa" dark chocolate. It resembled a clenched fist, hence the name.

But no one bought it. It was perfect: a bite of sweet old memories waiting for better times.

CLASSICO
ORIGINAL DARK
PERUGINA
Stabilimento:
S. Sisto (PG) - Italia

A way to have a little pleasure, a hint of luxury without feeling guilty. But no one bought it.

Fortunately, Giovanni Buitoni, Francesco's son, entered the scene. He had studied law in Germany, and now he was back, ready to rescue the family business and demonstrate his incredible marketing skills. First, banning the Cazzotto name: people needed something nice, sweet, and comfy. Not to order a punch! What would one like to ask the cute ladies behind the counters? A KISS!!!

Tags were immediately rewritten and showcased in the windows of the candy shops. People came in! They wanted a kiss from the mortified girl in the shop; one to take home; one for the wife and one for the lover; one to declare a blossoming love; one for mom, one for dad, and one for themselves! Bacio Perugina was the hugest success of the company. Ever!

Luisa wanted kisses too: to and from Giovanni. And apparently, once again, she got what she fancied. Legend says that the idea of the vellum with love quotes that still wraps the chocolates came from the habit of the two lovers sending each other passionate messages accompanying new formulas and recipes "to try".

But Giovanni's talent didn't end here. And Luisa's either. The treats were packaged in a silver aluminum foil decorated with blue lettering - and later with stars -: an apparent reference to Umbria's religious art tradition. Blue representing the sky, the water, serenity, peace - and consequently the Virgin Mary. Also, later, the color of the local, traditional art of ceramic. Baci Perugina were then advertised through the genius of Federico Seneca, one of the most excellent and most innovative Italian graphic designers. Federico took inspiration from Venetian Francesco Hayez's Il Bacio. The painting had become the symbol of Italian Romanticism in the previous century and was perfect for Baci Perugina.

It would become boring to list for you all the following successes of Perugina, and the Buitoni family. That will be a whole other story in a future issue. However, we are still to uncover Luisa's other gifts. For example, if you've ever tried a Rossana candy, you might want to join me in thanking her for my absolutely favorite Caramella.

But there's more. Luisa retired in the twenties and moved to a villa in the Umbrian hills, surrounded by plants and animals. Her favorite pets were angora rabbits. Day after day, with clothes full of rabbit hair, she wondered if that fur was spinnable. No hurting nor shearing would be admitted. So, she closed herself in the garage to experiment with a cruelty-free method, some sort of stripping. Sometime later, the same women who had worked for her at Perugina were called to arms: it was time to launch the Luisa Spagnoli fashion brand and the new angora knitwear.

37

PINTURICCHIO

If you've ever worked in a company or for a company, you've probably experienced how vital politics are. Sometimes even shadowing talent and hard work. If you say the wrong word, or you're unable to manage the moods of your boss or gossipy colleagues, then you'll be labeled. If you want to bring in novelty and innovation. If you want a project of yours to be approved and implemented. You'll have to walk a long and impervious road of diplomacy and negotiation. Not fair, but true. And even truer here in Italy where personal issues and sympathy are an integral part of office life. Some people don't get it. Or won't succumb, no matter what, to "that's the way life goes." Of those people, some get kicked out. Some are so gifted - and grumpy -, so indispensable, no one dares to mess with them. They survive in a jungle of extroversion. Many others opt for retiring and limiting their contacts with the external world. While a few others build their own kingdoms. Bernardino di Betto, born in Perugia in 1452, was one of them. His nickname, Pinturicchio, was given to underline his small frame: piccolo pintor, small painter. But he didn't mind and even signed many of his masterpieces with it. Although huge commissions from popes*, bishops and aristocratic families**, and even a place in the Cappella Sistina, his contemporaries had tepid opinions over his talents. And strongly negative ones over his person. Giorgio Vasari, critic and witness of the Renaissance art world, ridiculed him. Apparently, Pinturicchio, temporarily residing at a Franciscan monastery in Siena, wouldn't stop babbling about a troublesome old dresser in his room. Claims. Demands. Whining. One day the monks decided to silence him and remove it. In the process, it fell, broke, and five hundred gold coins capped the friar's feet! The treasure, of course, was retained by the monastery, while sourness brought the painter to death.

Not that he was a poor, miserable artist. Pinturicchio was rich. With his busy workshop and numerous assistants, he had acquired houses, villas, and lands in Umbria and nearby Tuscany. He was so wealthy he even paid his wife two-hundred-fifty florins for not having to see his mother-in-law! Unfortunately, although always based on gossipy sources, his personal life wasn't idyllic. At around fifty-nine, Pinturicchio fell ill, depending on his wife Grania for most of his basic needs. Neighbors reported hearing him begging for food.

Apparently, Grania and her lover, Il Paffa, had special plans.

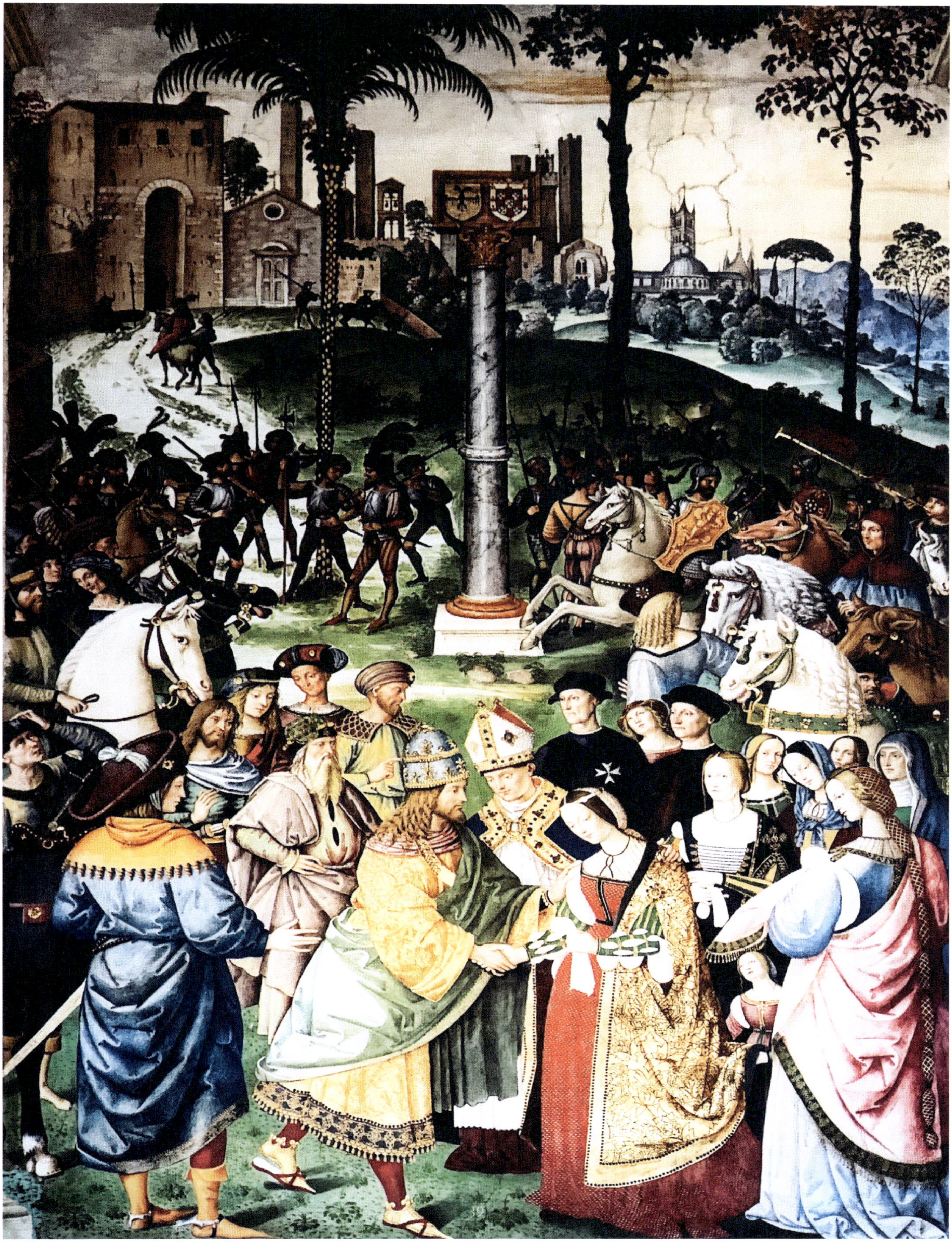

With no happy ending for either. The soldier of fortune later married the painter's daughter, Clelia. And the abandoned Grania excluded her daughter from her will.

Now that the gossipy moment has passed, let's concentrate on Pituricchio's style. It wasn't greatly appreciated by his fellow artists. Mainly, he was labeled as "out of fashion." He had little interest in storytelling and spiritual significance. And much more in chromatics, costumes, and landscaping. Resulting in a decorative, more than narrative, art. Plus, his landscapes were imaginative: fancily created and masterfully executed. Indeed, he is still called the more laic of all his contemporaries. As always, there's more. Together with Signorelli and Raffaello, he was one of the creators of the "Grottesche" art movement. Pinturicchio dedicated much of his time in Rome to visit the underground ruins - called Grotte (grottos), thus the name of the movement - of the Domus Aurea. Alone, and with the sole candlelight, he began replicating the decorative elements on the walls of Nero's residence. A mixture of hieroglyphs, Ovidio's Metamorphosis myths, gothic like monsters, and dionysian symbols. Pinturicchio and his fellows unmistakably enriched their executions with their styles and contaminations from their era. The religious iconography blended in, and the result was a decorative style made of hybrid zoomorphic, vegetable, and mythological elements***.

Then came the Council of Trent.

The Grotesque art was accused of provoking hallucinating blindness because of its absurd compositions. Of obscenity, irreverence, and, in a word, paganism. Mr. Vasari was part of the disrepute committee; surprised?

But Grottesche spread throughout Europe - the land of all-time lovers of transgression - and became pretty fashionable until the 19th century. Nevertheless, thanks to Vasari and others, Pinturicchio was relegated to a Renaissance B-list. It was only in the 19th and 20th centuries that more objective historians restored his name.

It makes me sad to think of how the opinions of others too often shadow your real you and your talents. Then I realize... It's always an unusual creature that captures my attention when traveling, visiting a museum, or browsing a book. If it has wings and hooves. If flames frame it. If it has a disturbing expression. If it is different. I stop. Sometimes it's a dragon. Or an angel. A pope, a peasant, or the Virgin Mary. If I perceive intensity, I fall in love and thank the artist for not bending to "that's the way life goes".

*Pinturicchio painted the Borgia apartments in the Vatican.
**Remember Pinturicchio's frescoes in the Libreria Piccolomini - the Siena issue? The picture here is from there.
*** In the next page, there's an example of the Grottesche style in Villa Farnesina, Rome.

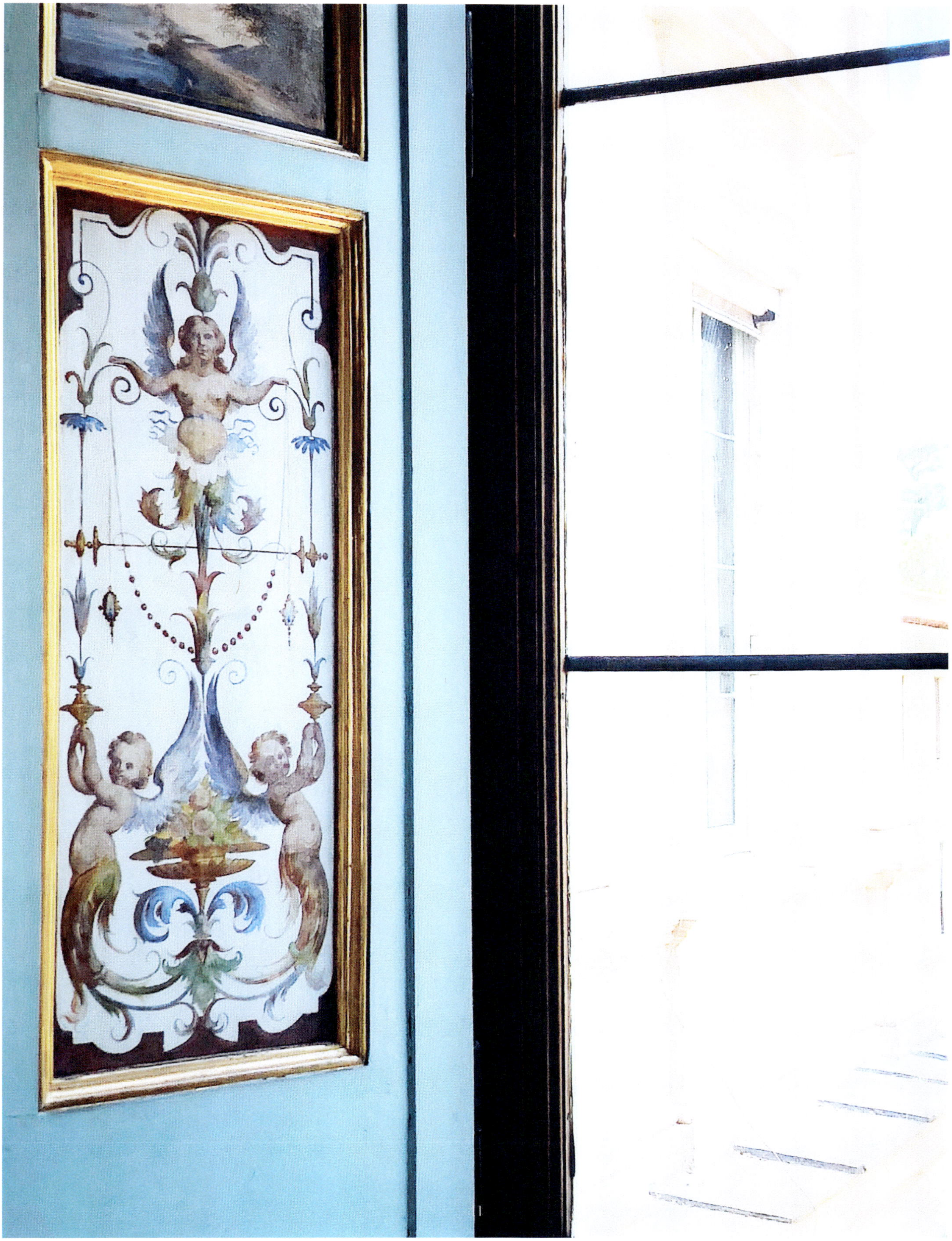

FARRO ALLA PERUGINA

As anticipated, legumes and cereals are very common and beloved by Umbrians. In Perugia, farro is cooked with tomatoes and a big piece of prosciutto. Actually, it would be a prosciutto bone that you boil to make broth and from which you tear off all the meat, once tender. But it is quite unrealistic to have at hand a prosciutto bone. A big piece of rich, fatty, and tasty Prosciutto is a more than decent alternative.

Ingredients for two:
150 gr (5.3 oz or 2/3 cup + 2 tablespoons) of farro
450 gr (15.9 oz or 1 + 3/4 cup + 2 tablespoons) of water
1/2 carrot
1/2 celery stalk
2 medium tomatoes - Roma or salad, or Pelati if out of season
1 thick slice of Prosciutto - about 50 gr (1.8 oz)
1/2 white or yellow onion
1 tablespoon of grated Pecorino cheese
salt

Peel the carrot and the onion.
Cut the tomatoes in four.
Pour the water into a medium pot, add the Prosciutto slice, carrot, onion, celery stalk, and tomatoes. Bring to a boil and simmer for twenty minutes.
Fetch the Prosciutto and finely chop it.
Filter the broth, keep the liquid, and discard the rest.
Return the broth to the pot, bring to a boil, add the farro, and a teaspoon of salt. Cook until well done. This should happen when the liquids have evaporated completely - about twenty to thirty minutes -, but you might need to add a quarter cup or so of water.
Once cooked, serve the farro topped with the Prosciutto trite and dusted with the Pecorino cheese.

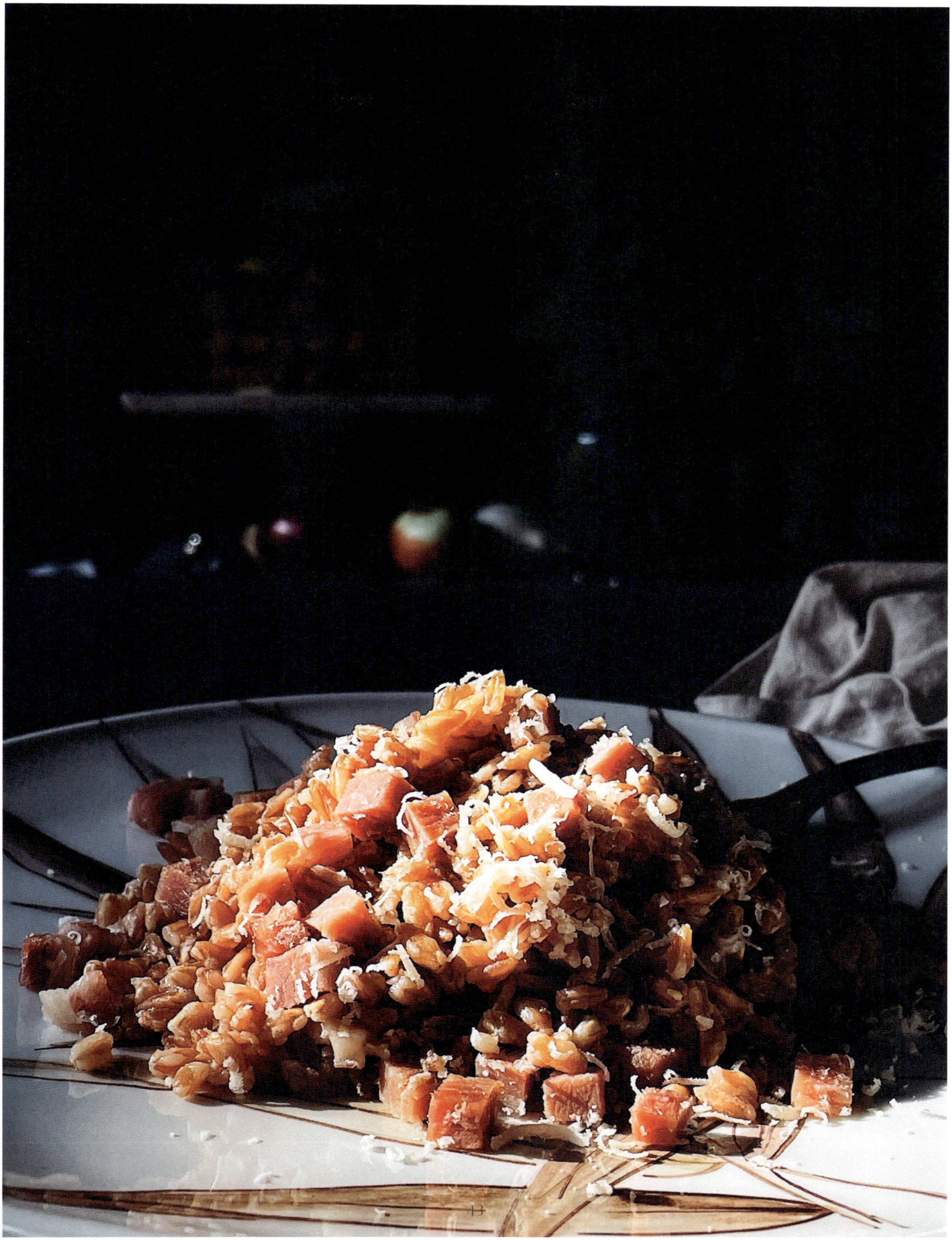

CARDI ALLA PERUGINA

Cardi, thistles, are called Gobbi in Umbria. It means hunchbacked. It is to recall the shape they assume when covered with soil to protect them from the cold: in search of light, they curve.
Gobbi Alla Perugina is a thistle version of the eggplant parmesan. Indeed, some also add mozzarella. The thistles are boiled, fried, then layered in a casserole, alternating meat ragu and abundant grated parmesan. So yes, it is not a light meal. Most often, it is prepared for Christmas. But despite that, I heard of an unexpected tradition: hiding a layer of Fettine Panate (fried veal breaded cutlets) inside the casserole!
To make things easier, you can clean and boil the thistles and make the tomato sauce the day ahead!

Ingredients for two:
400 gr (14 oz) of thistles
150 gr (5.3 oz) of ground beef, mixed beef and pork, or Italian sausage
2 tablespoons of all-purpose flour
1/4 white onion
2 canned tomatoes (Pelati)
a small piece of room-temperature butter to grease the casserole dish
1 lemon
2 cups of extra virgin olive oil + 1 tablespoon for the tomato sauce
about 4 tablespoons of grated parmesan cheese
salt and black pepper
one small casserole

Bring a big pot of salted water to a boil - about two liters (half a gallon) and one tablespoon of salt. Clean the thistles by removing the leaves and accurately peeling off the green outer fiber. Cut them in six centimeters/two and a half inches pieces and place them in a pot with water and a lemon squeezed in - to avoid them from blackening.
Drain them, toss them in the boiling water, and cook them for thirty minutes. Discard the water and pat them dry with a kitchen cloth. Transfer them to a mixing bowl, sprinkle them with the flour and shake to coat them well. Discard the extra flour.
Heat two cups of olive oil in a small pot. Toss in the thistles and fry them until golden - about five minutes. Line a plate with kitchen paper, remove the thistles with tongs, and transfer them to the plate in one layer. Add another layer of paper to adequately absorb the extra grease.
Peel and finely chop the onion. Use a fork to crush the tomatoes.
Heat a tablespoon of olive oil in a medium pan and sauté the onion until translucent - about five minutes. Add the tomatoes, the ground beef (if using sausage peel and husk the meat), a pinch of salt, and a few grinds of pepper - about five. Mix, cover, and cook for fifteen minutes.
Preheat the oven to 200°C/390°F.
Grease the casserole dish with butter. Distribute a layer of thistles. Cover them with a spoonful or two of the beef ragu, then a tablespoon of grated parmesan. Add another layer of thistles, one of sauce, and one of parmesan. Go on until you finish the ingredients. On average, you should get two layers. Lastly, cover the surface with an extra layer of grated parmesan.
Bake the casserole for twenty minutes. You should get a soft crust on the surface.
Serve your Gobbi Alla Perugina hot!

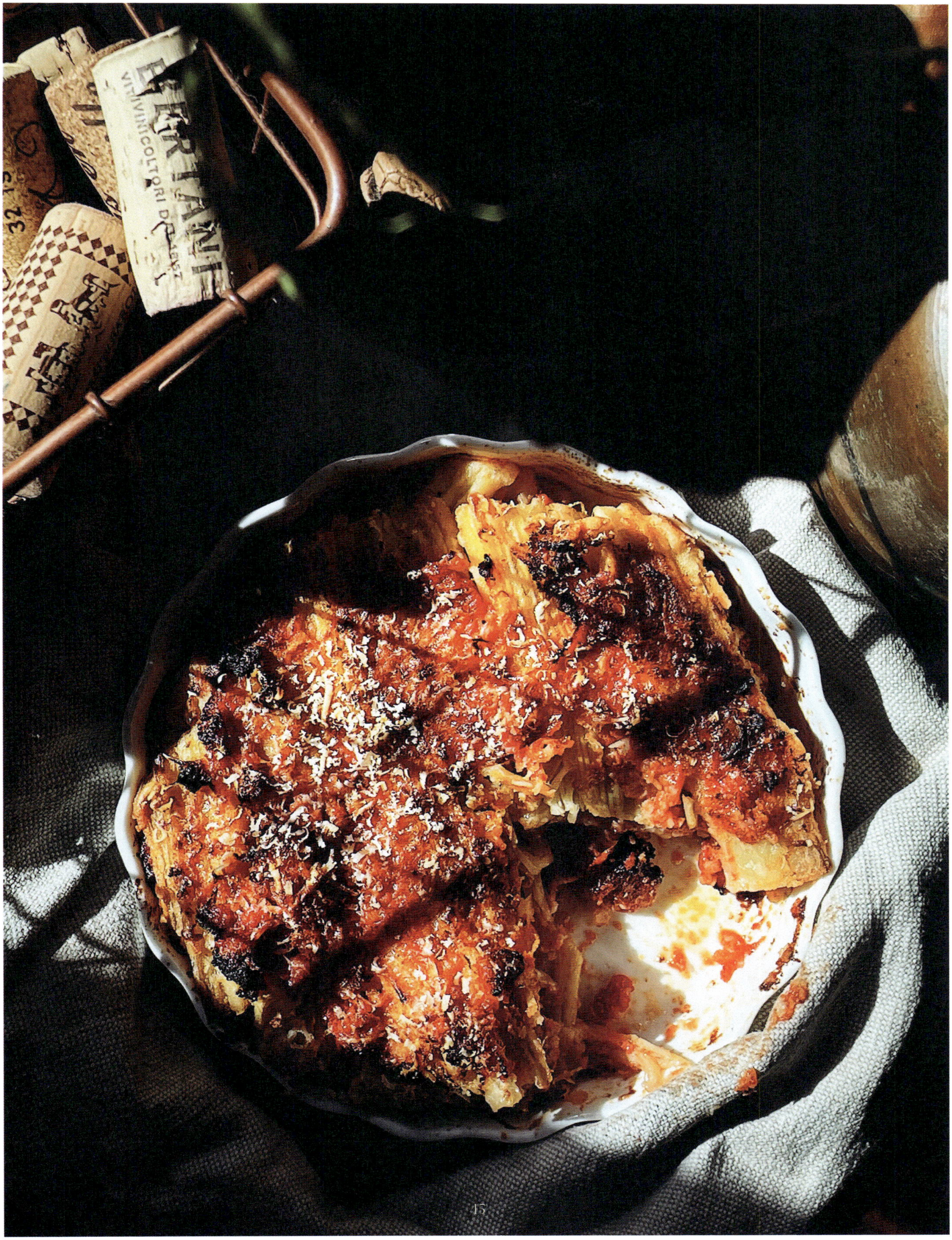

TORELLO ALLA PERUGINA

Torello Alla Perugina is an ancient recipe created to recover the meat used for the stock or broth. The meat that had lost most of its flavor was surmounted by a creamy condiment made of chicken liver, herbs, and spices. If you've ever tried Crostino Umbro or Toscano, you are well aware of how tasty and delicious chicken liver pate is. I sometimes give up a meal in order to eat only toasted bread and Patè Di Fegatini. Nowadays, we don't need to rescue boiled meat, but cook it and enjoy its flavor furtherly enriched with the spread.

Ingredients for two:
300 gr (10.5 oz) of Girello (Eye of Round Beef)
60 gr (2 oz) of chicken liver - ask your butcher to clean them
1/4 onion
1/2 carrot
1/2 celery stalk
3 sage leaves
1/4 cup of dry white wine
1 anchovy
1 teaspoon of capers
1/4 lemon
extra virgin olive oil
salt and black pepper
kitchen twine

If needed, clean the chicken livers: place them in a bowl and soak them for about thirty minutes in water and a bit of lemon juice. Then pat them dry.
Afterward, lay out and unfold each piece so that they are flat. With the help of a sharp knife, trim the meat away from the connective tissue - white or pinkish -, and possibly coagulated blood (the blackish parts). Cut them into pieces and set them aside.
Sprinkle the beef with a pinch of salt and a few grinds of pepper, then tie it with kitchen twine every two inches.
Peel and coarsely chop the onion and the carrot. Coarsely slice the celery stalk. Place the capers in a cup and cover them with water. Set them aside for later.
In a medium pan, heat two tablespoons of olive oil. Add the onion, carrot, and celery stalk and sautè, medium heat, until the onion becomes translucent - five to ten minutes. Add the meat and sear all sides for a minute or so. Pour in the wine and a quarter cup of water, toss in the sage leaves, cover, and cook for twenty minutes.
Add the cleaned chicken liver, sprinkle with a pinch of salt and a few grinds of pepper - about five grinds - and cook for twenty minutes more on medium heat.
Transfer the beef to a cutting board.
Pour the cooking liquids into a grinder. Add the livers, anchovy, and squeezed capers. Trite until creamy.
Slice the meat by half an inch or so and plate the slices surmounted by the creamy condiment.

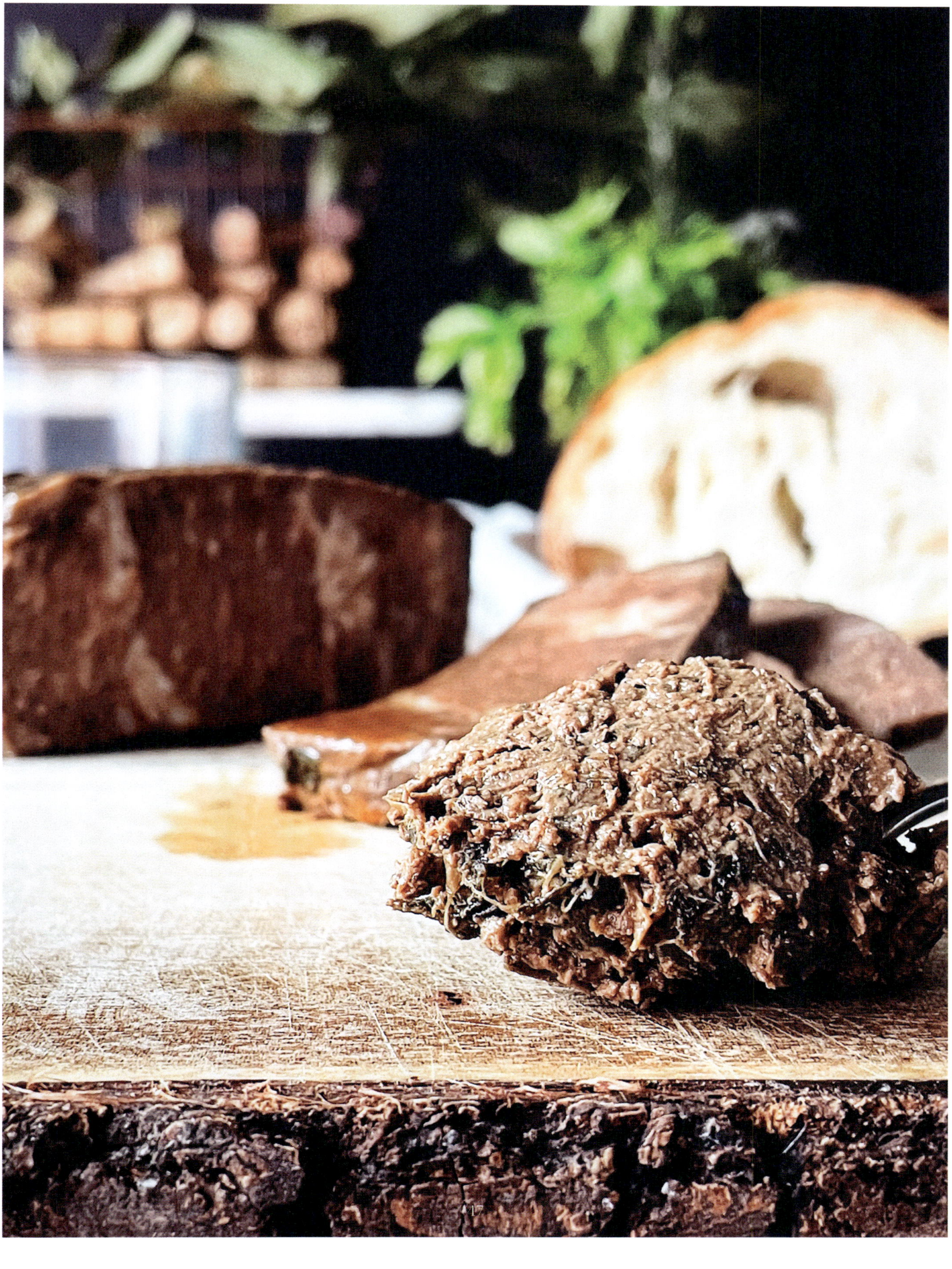

GUBBIO

If I were Cappuccetto Rosso, Little Red Riding Hood, I'd move to Gubbio after the dramatic and traumatizing experience with the Wolf. I'd drag nonna out of the woods and furnish a cute brick house inside the protective, thick walls. I'd give her all she needed: stove, rocking chair, membership to the local book club, but ban any adventure out of the town. I'd choose Gubbio because it would make me feel safe, secure, and sheltered. After a while, say a few decades, I'd even be ready for another adventure. Because I'd have this magical place to return to. Bad things are part of life. But when you are here, it feels more acceptable. The lucent stones of the walls infuse courage in you. Not armed-to-the-teeth courage, but strength. The calm strength of vitality, of a good night's sleep, of having been nestled and nurtured. You feel capable of climbing the city tower and pushing the three bells with your entire body to create that potent, vital sound that alerts the city it is time to celebrate. Celebrate what? Life!

The last time we landed in Gubbio, on our way to another region of Italy, I couldn't believe my eyes. It came out of an enchanted mirror. Or wardrobe, or puddle. As it was Christmas, the enchantment was duplicated. The walls and windows were elegantly decorated. The tiny bodegas, graciously showcased truffles, fabrics, and wooden toys. People, tourists as well, moved slower and smiled more. All I felt like doing was swirling and hopping. I wished I had a red cape*. Round and wide enough to sway during a pirouette. I would run thrice around the Bargello fountain and gain my insane certificate**. I also wished to spend a few months there, to relish the joys of winter. A cozy fireplace and a wool blanket. Tons of books and hot chocolate daily. Truffle pasta and day-long roasted meat. Vin brulè, mulled wine, on the weekends. A knitting set and an easel, brushes, and acrylics. And long walks holding roasted chestnuts in gloves I wouldn't mind dirtying. And a magic one-week diet just before Spring knocked on the door.

*Red as Little Red Riding Hood and as dressed are the Maestri Del Silenzio (the Masters of Silence), Gubbio's bell ringers, readers of the silent tempo.

**Legend says that if you run around the 16th-century fountain, you'll go insane. A citizen must accompany you and then baptize you. Then you can claim - buy - your "Matto (madman) di Gubbio" license. There might be a scientific base: traces of the highly toxic iridium in surrounding rock formations.

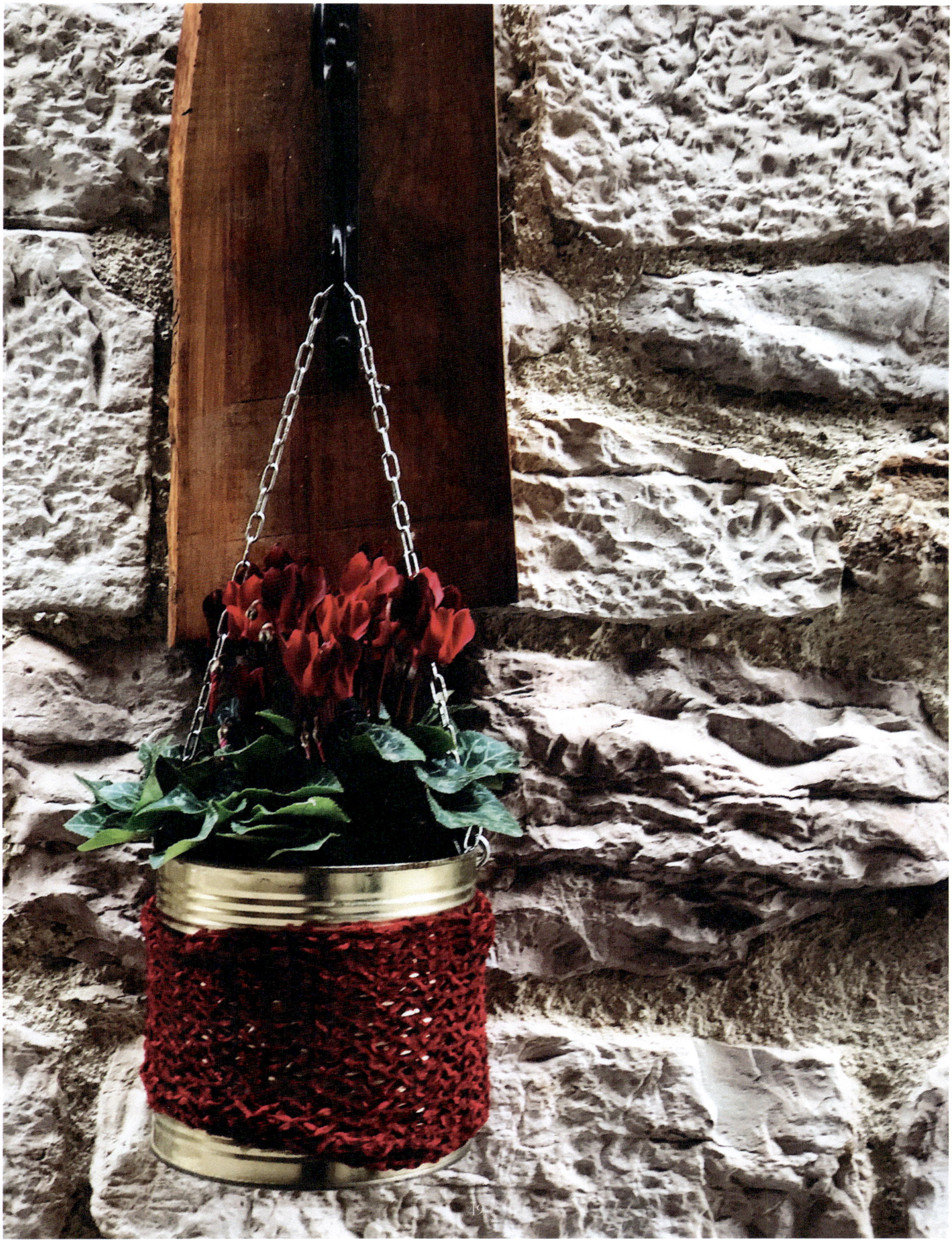

FESTA DEI CERI

So, as mentioned earlier, in Gubbio, you can get the Madness License. But I, who consider myself decently folly, don't think I could measure up. And definitely not fast enough. My madness is more introspective, apparently calm, hysterical inside. It's cerebral, rarely instinctive. Eugubini, instead, are crazy in a frantic, irrational way, and they are insane altogether and all in the same way. Quoting and distorting Tolstoy: "Happy fools are all alike; every unhappy fool is unhappy in its own way." At least in mid-May for the Festa Dei Ceri.

It's all about running. Running downhill. Running uphill. And pushing. Violently pushing one another.

Sant'Ubaldo, the city's patron, is celebrated on May 15th. Ubaldo was the bishop of the town in 1129. Through brilliant military strategies, he could scare off the troops of the eleven cities that had allied with Perugia against Gubbio. His curricula also included great inclination towards miracle-working and exceedingly effective exorcism rites.

Celebrations begin the night before the festivity. Locals go drinking plentiful amounts of wines in taverns. Reaching a state of Dionysian rapture. To grow into religious ecstasy, a believer would say. To celebrate the goddess Cerere, a pagan, would respond.

You can judge for yourself.

They dance in the streets. Bands play. They shout, run and sing. They splash in the Bargello fountain. Maybe to re-baptize themselves and validate their insanity for one more year. They fall and swirl. They laugh.

The next day, they gather in the streets for various communing rituals and finally for the Corsa Dei Ceri, which is just the climax of the almost month-long celebration. Including children running around the city with miniature - but not so small - Ceri carried on their shoulders. A game and a commitment for the future.

Three statues, Sant'Ubaldo, San Giorgio, and Sant'Antonio, are placed on giant Ceri. Their name and tradition derive from the candles the population lighted on the day Sant'Ubaldo died. These giant wooden twin prisms are decorated with oil-painted fabrics. No religious figures but only arabesques and branches. Men, women, and kids beat their palms on the wooden mastodons reminding more of an ancestral rite than a prayer.

Three teams, one dressed in yellow to honor Ubaldo, patron of stonemasons, one in blue to honor Giorgio, patron of merchants, and one in black for Antonio, patron of donkey keepers, raise the Ceri.

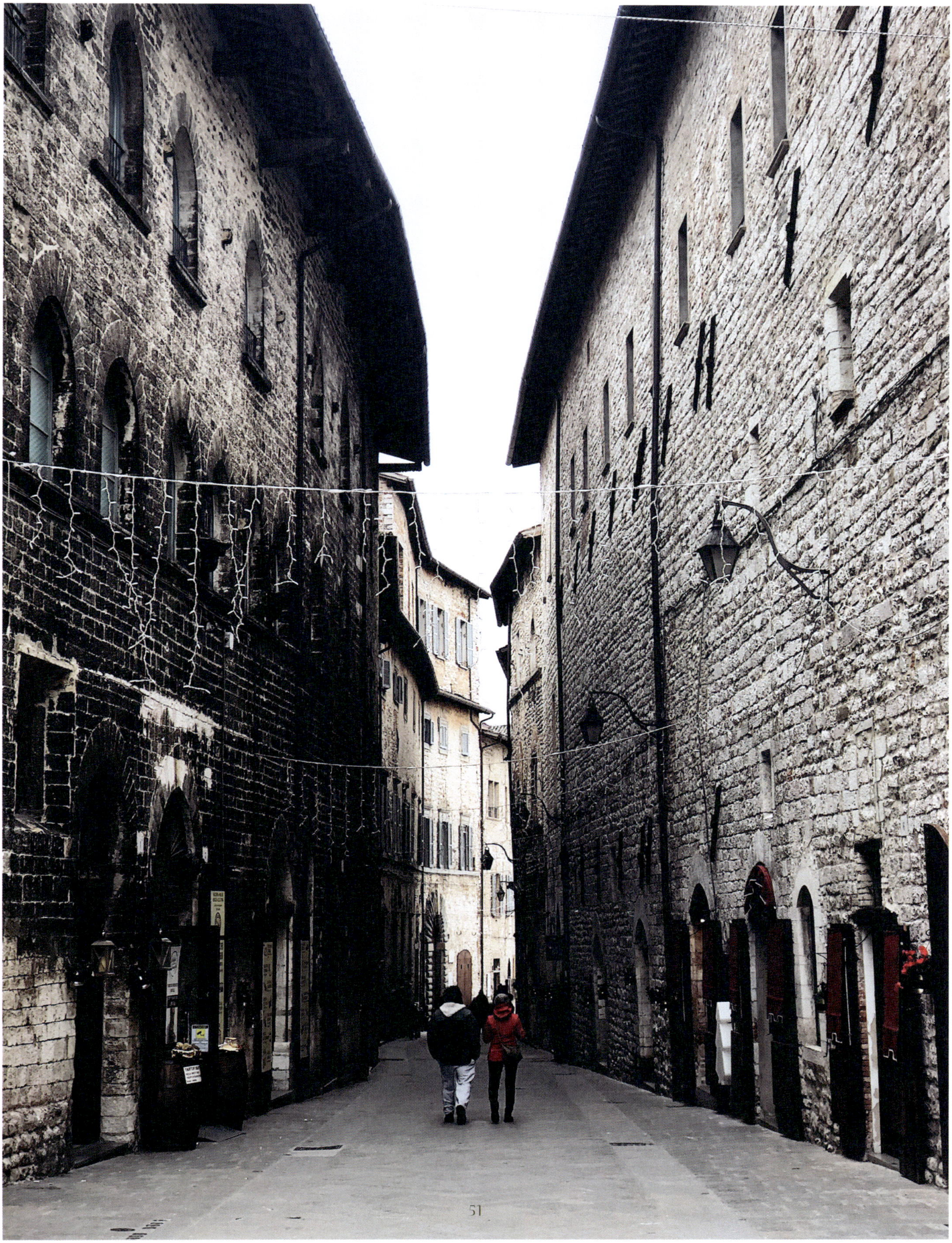

Pour profuse amounts of water from in-palette decorated giant jugs. What a surprise: another quite apparent reference to ancient agricultural rites. And the race begins. First in a circle, in front of the palace, and then downhill at maximum, dangerous, furious speed. During the noncompetitive run – perplexed? Sant'Ubaldo is always the first who can access the final destination –, new holders take over, always running, so in a very rude, shouldering way.

They cross the town and cover three routes, with short pauses in between. Time to refuel with wine pouring from the city fountains and cakes offered by the ladies. Time to salute the mayor, elder Ceraioli, and other prominent figures.

Part one is done.

Part two consists of the same run, only uphill, up to Sant'Ubaldo's Eremo. More pushing, more sprains, more sweating. And a final choral cry of relief once the Ceri are let fall but caught by others like in one of those nineteen-nineties teamworking retreats.

I can't stress enough the vitality and relentless pace in every moment of the day. Brisk eyes, sudden gestures, fast-talking. Anyone not insane would experience the symptoms of epilepsy. So, what do you say? Is the festivity dedicated to the saint or the goddess? Or is it one more way for us humans to vent fatigue, frustration, sadness, and stress?

Like it is for the women who despair at Taranto's processions.

Like it is for the folly Sienese at the horse Palio.

Like it is for that fury tumult in the soccer stadiums.

Curiosity: another Festa Dei Ceri is held in Jessup, Pennsylvania. Imported by Italian immigrants, of course!

53

PATE' ALL'EUGUBINA

I can't think of a better introduction than my complete devotion to this poor cuisine masterpiece. As mentioned earlier, I'd rather eat two, three, five servings of toasted bread spread with this chicken liver patè than many, many other dishes. There are many recipes, both in Umbria and Tuscany. This is All'Egubina, the Gubbio way.

Ingredients for two to four - one, if you'll love it as I do:
200 gr (7 oz) of chicken liver
1/2 garlic clove
1 juniper berry
2 sage leaves
2 tablespoons of white wine vinegar
extra virgin olive oil
salt
black pepper

The butcher should sell you the livers already clean. If not, place them in a bowl and soak them for about thirty minutes in water and a bit of lemon juice. Then pat them dry.
Afterward, lay out and unfold them so that they are flat. With the help of a sharp knife, trim the meat away from the connective tissue - white or pinkish -, and, eventually, the coagulated blood (the blackish parts).
Cut the meat in medium chunks and set it aside.
Peel and finely chop the garlic clove.
Heat two tablespoons of olive oil in a medium pan. Sautè the garlic over medium heat for about five minutes or until golden. Toss in the juniper berry and the sage leaves and brown them for a couple of minutes.
Add the liver in pieces, a pinch of salt, and a few grinds of pepper (about five). Stir for about five minutes to seal all the sides of the meat.
Pour in the vinegar and cook, low heat, about ten minutes more. More or less the time it takes for the livers to cook properly, release liquids, and for the latter to evaporate.
Transfer all the pan's content to a blender, add two tablespoons of olive oil, and pulse until creamy. You might need to add a tablespoon or two of olive oil to reach the desired consistency, which is grainy but spreadable. Taste for salt.

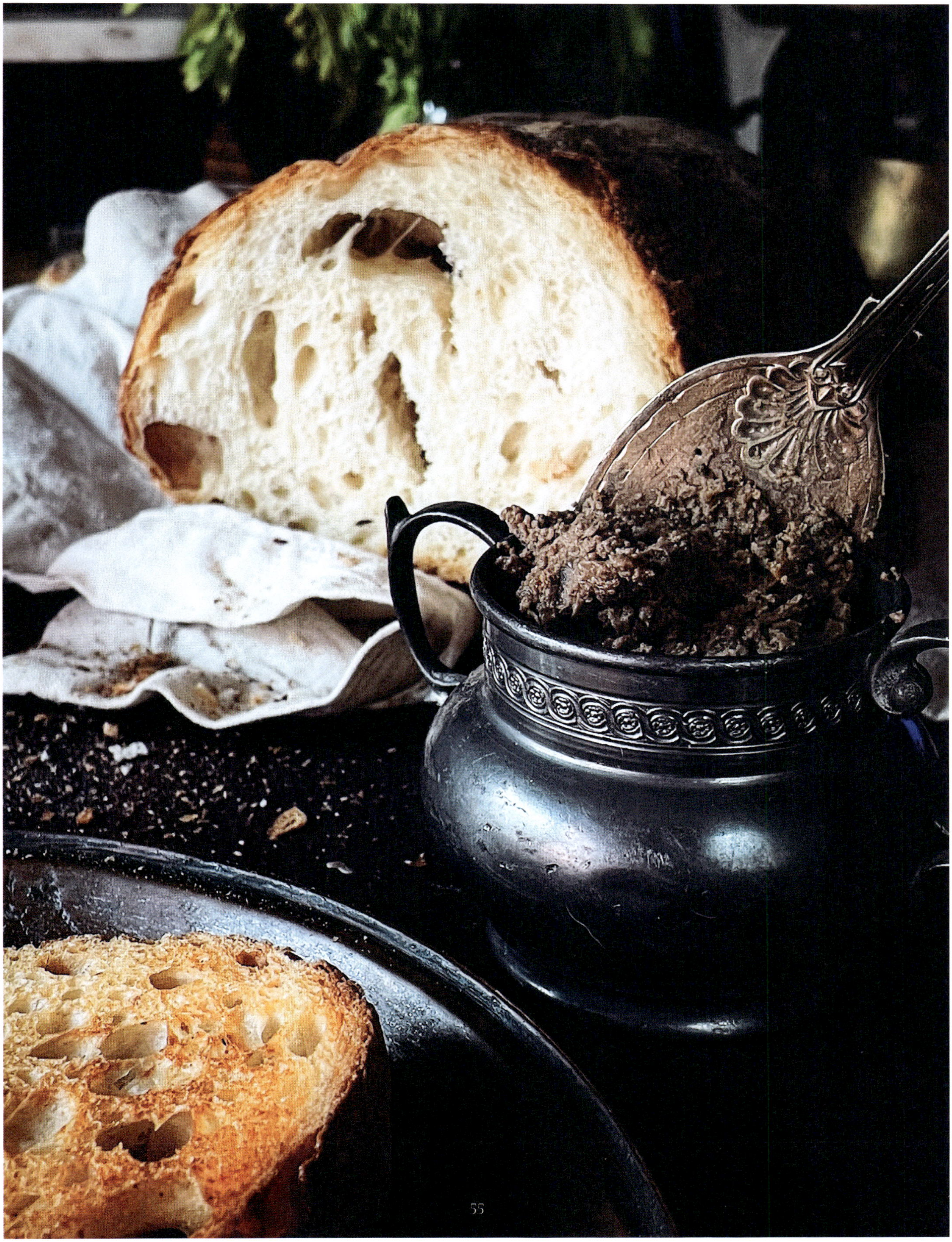

ACQUACOTTA DI GUBBIO

Here's another shared recipe with Tuscany: Acquacotta, cooked water. Again, a way to use stale bread and transform it into a nourishing, comforting bread soup. I've seen dozens of recipes, as many as the little towns scattered around the two regions. There are probably others in the areas I still need to explore. But for now, I can tell you this is Gubbio's recipe.

Ingredients for two:
500 gr (17.6 oz) of chicory greens (dandelion greens)
1 garlic clove
50 gr (1.8 oz) of Pancetta
1/2 onion
4 slices of stale rustic Italian bread
extra virgin olive oil
salt and black pepper

Clean the chicory from dirt and remove the base and the older leaves. Wash and drain.
Bring a big pot of salted water to a boil - about two liters (half a gallon) and one tablespoon of salt.
Toss in the leaves and cook them for fifteen minutes.
In the meantime, peel and finely chop the garlic and the onion. And finely dice the Pancetta.
In a medium pan, heat a teaspoon of olive oil and add the Pancetta. Sautè it until translucent and a little crispy. Add the garlic and onion and cook them until golden.
Drain the chicory, keep half a cup of the water, and squeeze the leaves.
Carefully transfer the chicory to the pan. Bring heat to high and sautè the veggies, constantly stirring to coat them completely with the flavored oil, for about five minutes.
Place the bread slices in two serving bowls. Drizzle each slice with a tablespoon or two of the vegetable cooking water. Cover with the sautéed vegetables. Serve hot!

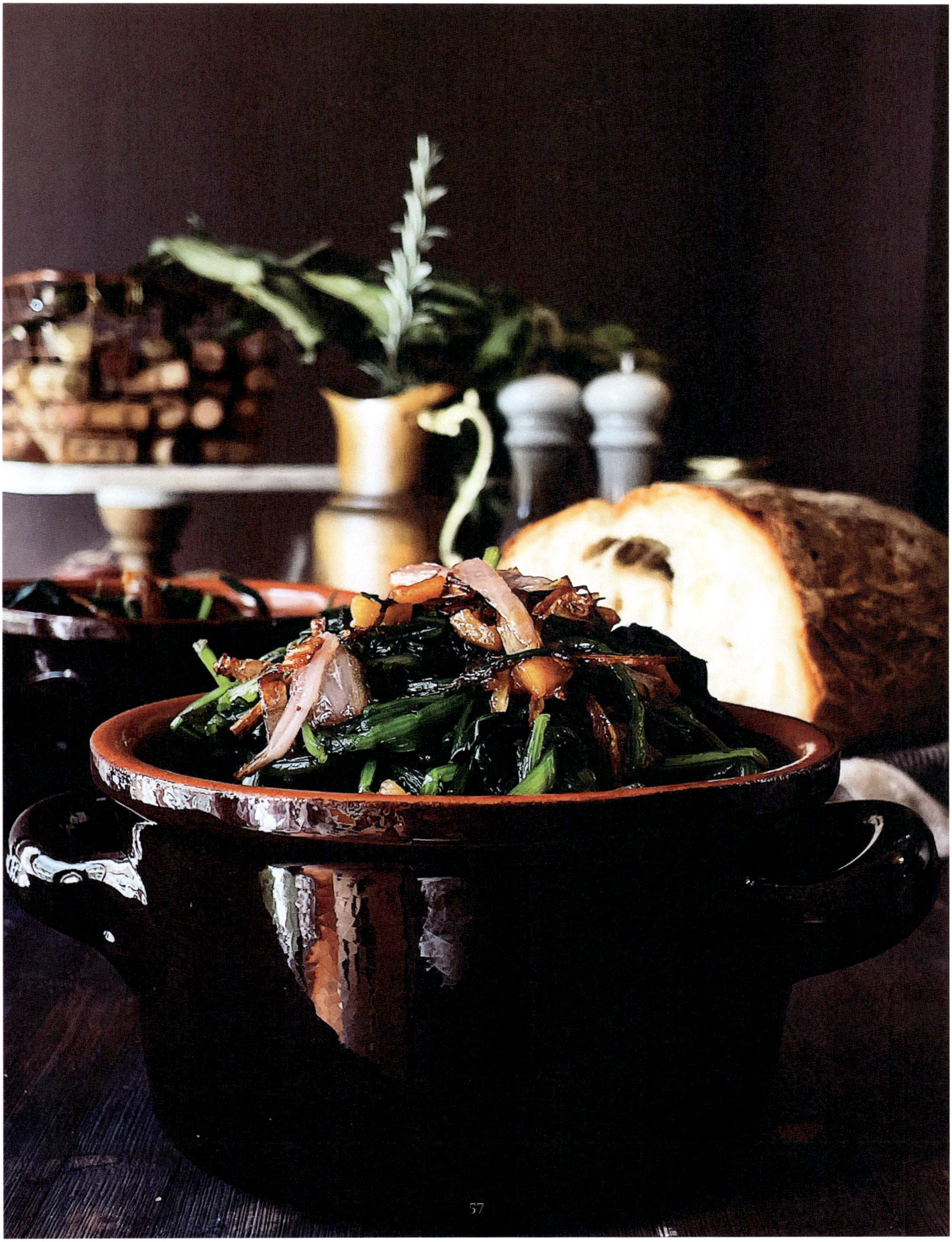

IMBRECCIATA

You might remember that an ancient New Year's Eve tradition here in Italy is to put a handful of wheat grains in your pocket. Cereals symbolize abundance for the coming year, as well as many other ingredients on the table. Lentils at midnight, to name another.
In Gubbio and the surrounding territories, they go a little further and prepare, for the lunch of January 1st, a soup with every cereal and legume leftover in the pantry: the Imbrecciata.
Good luck and prosperity in every form!
Imbrecciata is earlier than Ancient Rome. Centuries ago, the soup was served dry, almost a polenta. We have proof in the Tavole Eugubine (Tabulæ Iguvinæ): seven bronze tablets written in ancient Umbro - the idiom of the native Umbri. The religious inscriptions have treasured most of the acts and rites of the early city and the recipe of the first Imbrecciata.

Ingredients for two:
200 gr (7 oz or about 1 cup) of mixed legumes and cereals - in this case: lentils, pearl barley, pearl spelt, dry split broad beans, and lentils
1 garlic clove
1/4 white or yellow onion
1 small fresh rosemary sprig
2-3 sage leaves
1 tablespoon of fresh parsley
1 small sprig of marjoram
250 gr (7 oz or 1 cup) of tomato paste (Passata) or peeled tomatoes (Pelati)
2 tablespoons of extra virgin olive oil
salt and black pepper

If you are using different cereals and legumes, check if they need to be soaked overnight. In this case, place them in separate bowls and cover them with water. Let them rehydrate overnight. For the ones I indicate in the ingredients list, soaking is not needed: they're all easily cooked. Place them in a medium pot instead, cover them with water plus a couple of inches, and bring to a boil over medium heat. Lower to medium/low heat and cook until everything is fork tender - about forty minutes. You may need to add a quarter or half a cup of water to end the cooking.
Peel and finely chop the onion and the garlic clove. Finely chop the parsley and set it aside for later. Heat the olive oil in another pot, add the chopped onion and garlic, and sauté until golden, about five minutes over medium heat.
Add the tomato paste and half a teaspoon of salt, mix and bring to a boil. Cook ten minutes at medium/low heat.
Once cooked, transfer the cereals and legumes to the tomato sauce pot, add the rosemary sprig, the marjoram and sage leaves, and the chopped parsley. Stir and cook, medium/low heat, for twenty minutes.
Taste for salt and serve the Imbrecciata hot, sprinkled with a few drops of olive oil and a few grinds of pepper. Accompany it with toasted bread and be delighted by its simple gloriousness!

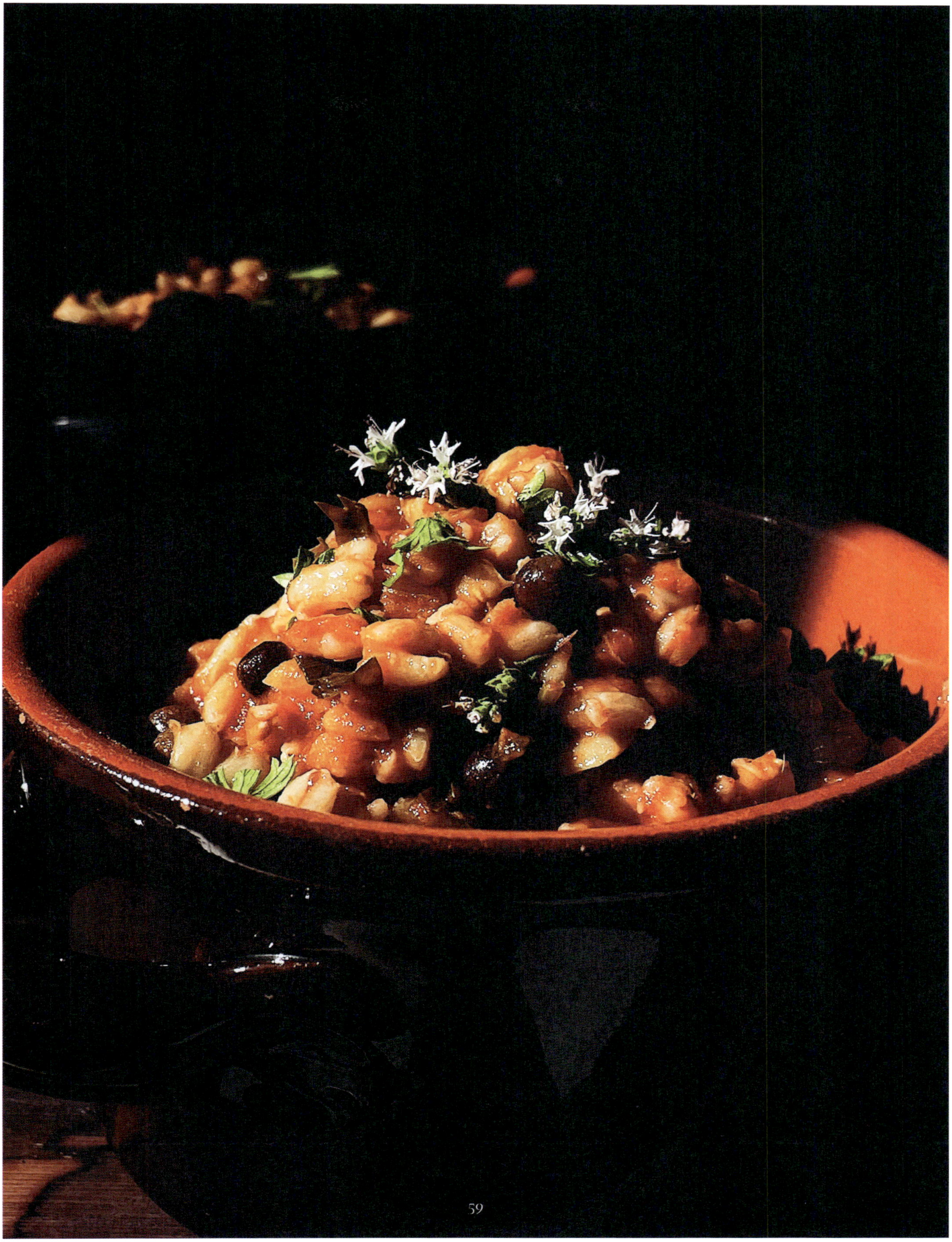

ORVIETO

If I were to spend a winter nestled next to the chimney, listening to stories and legends, I'd spend it in Orvieto.

A historian, a short man with a long beard responsible for the public library, would illuminate me, telling me the story of the city. Once a strategic and prominent headquarter of the Etruscan cities league, then the city of the Popes: alternative fortress residence to Rome.

Another evening would be spent with a timid, eyeglasses and comforting cashmere scarf, researcher. He'd let me know, avoiding eye contact at first, then letting me in his bright eyes and sharp intelligence, about Orvieto's academy, the Accademia Dei Misti. Instead of meager historical data, he'd lead me through intrigues and mysteries. With his mixed Tuscan, Roman, and Umbria accent, he'd say something like: "Why would Paolo Pietrantonio, the first prince, accept the protection of Cristina, queen of Sweden, for the academy? Rendering it public by adopting her two-palm arch emblem! All this after, years before, she had assassinated his father, Gian Rinaldo II Monaldeschi. Her lover and favorite. But also the author of some letters - which content we ignore - that led him to a horrible execution. Could it be true that his son was her lover too? Could we find an explanation in the queen's and the academy's interest for alchemy?"

I'd certainly catch a cold one day or another. One evening, my neighbor, a tall curved lady, wearing gloves, hat, scarf, and a shawl, would knock on my door, carrying a blanket, a lace napkin for me, and a bottle of Orvietan. She'd invite herself in, take a seat, cover herself furtherly with her thick quilt, and smile at me: ciao, bella! While pouring both a tiny glass of the sweetish liquor, she'd say: "this, bella, is a curative remedy. Invented by Girolamo Ferranti (called the Orvietano). It is a miraculous elixir. Drink, drink! The secret recipe has been handed down only to Orvietani. It is ours. But we love to share. Drink, bella, drink! Even Louis XIV, Il Re Sole, loved it!"

"Do you know the story of Romilda? Oh, that poor little creature. But astute! Luckily for her." Romilda met Polidoro Polidori in Tuscany, her homeland. She was a nurse; he was a wounded soldier. She took care of him; he took her home with him. At the beginning, they were a happy newlywed couple. They spent long and lazy days at his family country house. Kissing, walking around, gardening, and raising carrier pigeons.

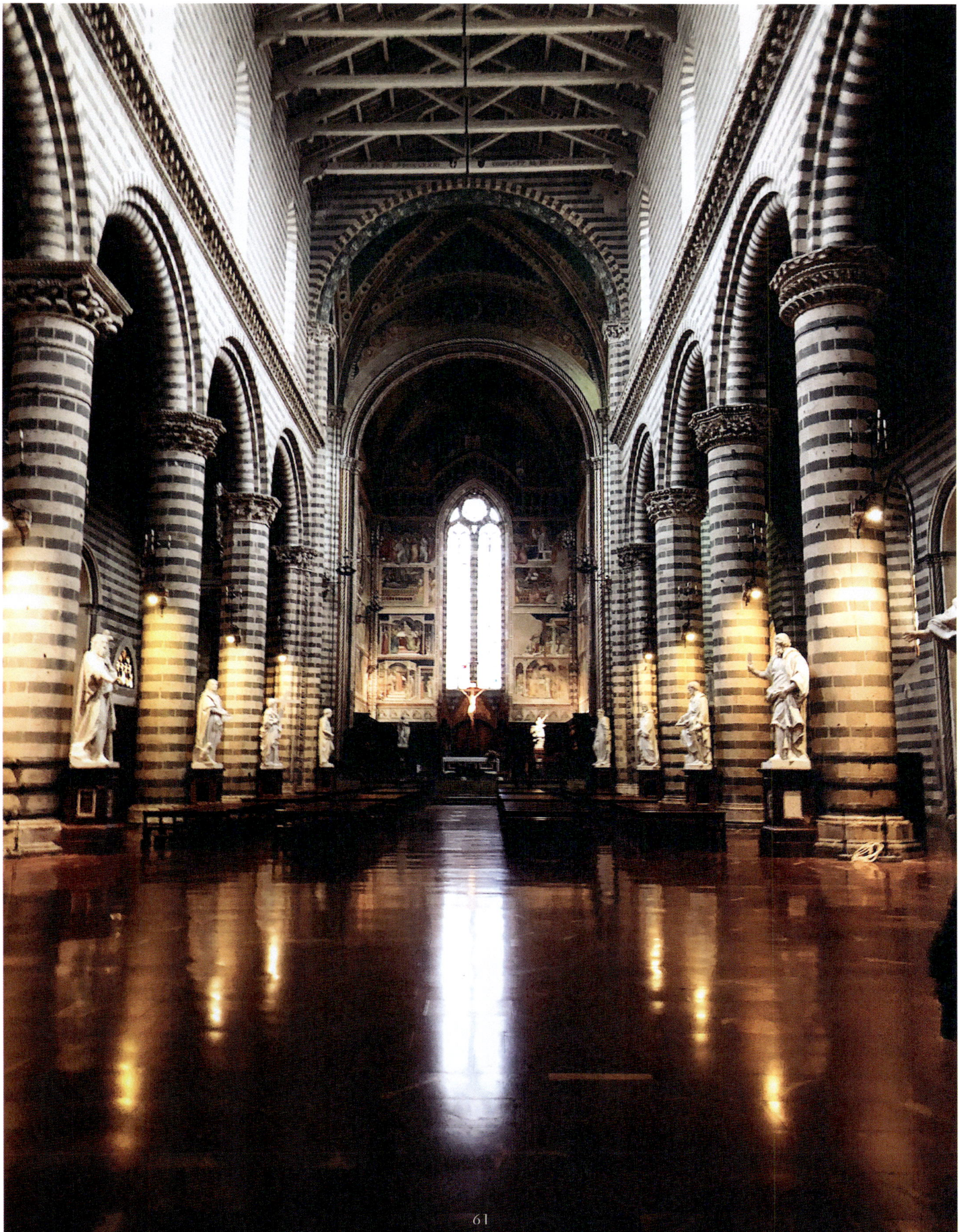

Those birds were her passion.

But with time, leisure failed. Days were too long. The sole company of her groom wasn't enough. The bells and voices of city life urged her. Boredom pushed her.

In the end, she convinced Polidoro to move to the family city home, the Tower Polidori.

For a while, she enjoyed her new life quite much. Too much, some thought. Her beauty wouldn't pass unnoticed, and surely not her vitality and passion. Word spread, glances became insolent, and as always happens, furious jealousy and incapacity to face other men condemned her. Her spouse locked her in the tower, denying her any socialization. She spent her days alternating cries to playing music, singing and lacemaking.

"See why I gifted you the lace napkin, bella? It is a traditional craft of Orvieto!"

Romilda spent her days in the tower with the only company of her pigeons. Her husband could come and go. Live his life, see his friends, go hunting, go drinking, participate in city events... But one day, he returned home - probably a little tipsy - and found no one and nothing but crumbles, feathers, and a half-finished lace. Romilda had been flown away by her birds! Gone forever. With the help of those damn little creatures! Why? Why? Why? The fumes of alcohol didn't let him decipher reality: Romilda had secretly made a mold from his keys, and one of the birds had simply delivered it to her family.

Another night, I'd find Marta, the blonde angelic girl from the top floor, crying in the hallway. "I'll throw myself down the cliff, just like Livio!" After accepting a hot chocolate and a moment of tranquilizing silence, she'd share with me her evils of love. Her mother wouldn't let her date Marco - "a deadbeat". And her cousin had betrayed her, recounting of the time she "marinated" school* with the boy. "Just like Livio, just like Livio!"

When I'd ask who Livio was, Marta would tell me the story of the local Romeo and Juliet. Livio, from a wealthy Roman family of merchants, had met Livia, from Rome as well, at a wedding. But his cousins were bandits and had some sort of unfinished business with him. So, at another big family gathering, they had poisoned the girl, condemning her to three days of agony. Livio, who was in Rome for some family business, came back just in time to experience the traumatic feelings of his beloved dying in his arms. Blinded by fury, he killed his cousins and threw himself from his palace. In his hands, his family found a sprig of hawthorn, although out of its blooming season. The plant was considered the "flower of the bride".

Ever since, every year on the date of the tragedy, a hawthorn sprig flourishes.

At the end of her tale, I'd convince the delicate girl to accompany me, on the next day, to search for that sprig. I'd be sure we'd meet many other Marcos and Livios on our way.

One night, I'd receive the visit of a devote and her daughter.

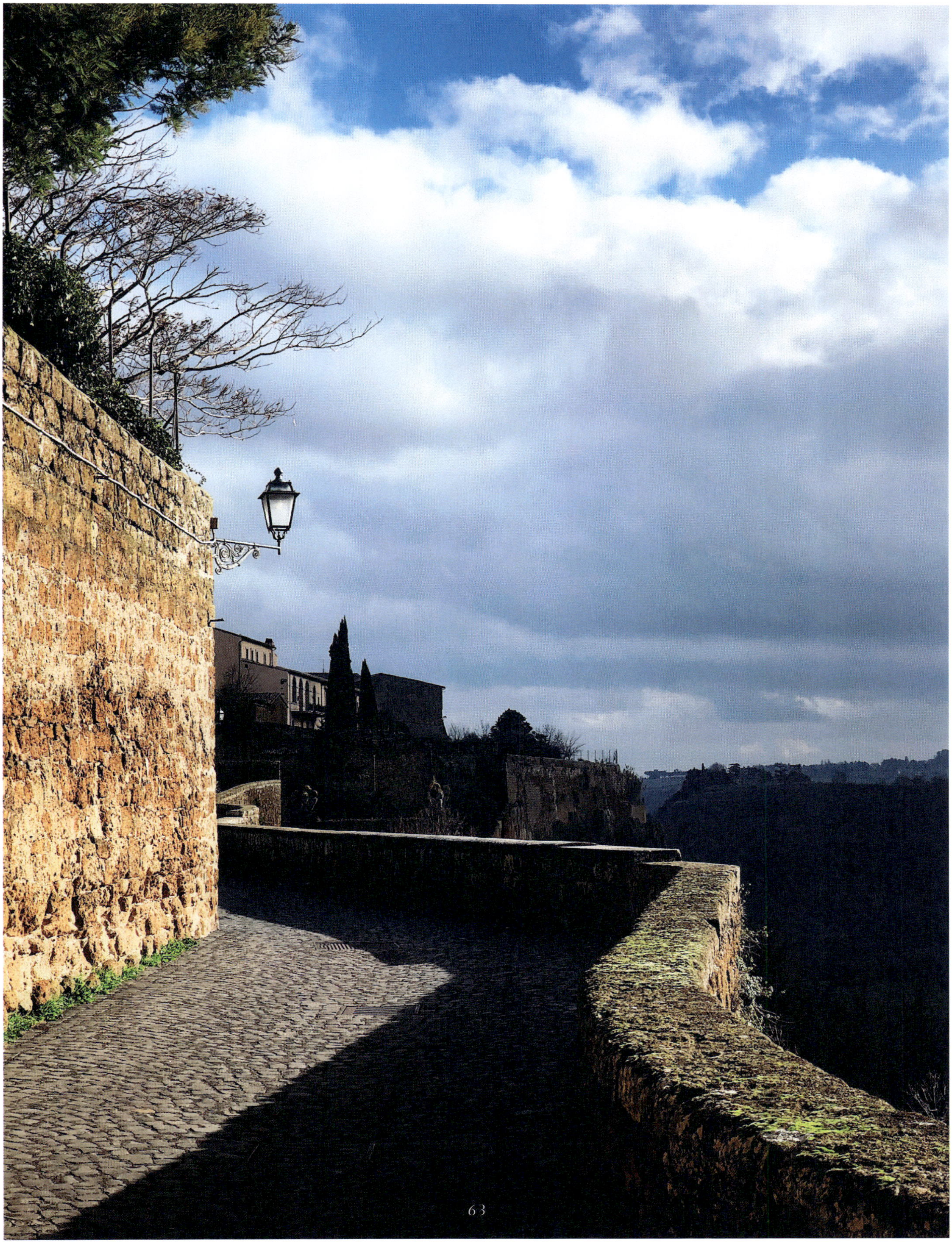

The women, hearing of the visitor who likes to listen to the stories of Orvieto, would introduce herself and her intent: "I must be sure you know the story of our cathedral. And that you hear it from proper voices."

She'd then tell me about Pietro Di Praga, a priest in the middle of a religious crisis.

He had begun to doubt that the host truly contained the body of Jesus Christ. It was 1263, and at the time, the place to find answers was still Rome. So, he embarked himself on a holy pilgrimage. On his way to the religious capital, he stopped for a night in Bolsena. After getting up early, he offered to say mass to the congregation. But during the consecration of the bread, the host began to bleed. Incredulous and frightened, he wrapped it in a cloth and hid it.

Pope Urbano IV was in Orvieto in those days, so the priest decided to take there the holy host.

"All his doubts were cleared, and the pope built the cathedral to treasure the relic".

I'd politely smile and thank the lady for her precious story. The woman would stand up straight, as straight as she was seated, and direct herself to the door, repeating how pleased she was, how relieved to know she – a believer! – had been my source of information.

A murmur, a puff I would hardly catch, would come out of her bottomed up, almost strangled daughter: "Marcescens bacteria". After saying goodnight, I would promptly google it.

Google would correct my spelling and inform me that S. Marcescens is a bacterium that forms, in warm climates, on bread, polenta, potatoes, and other starchy foods. It produces a bright orange to deep-red pigment.

I'd smirk. But I'd be happy to have one more anecdote in my collection.

On my last night in Orvieto, someone would knock on my door. A bald, tall, rosy-cheek man would ask permission to invite me out for a glass of Orvieto Rosso and a chat. "I waited until the last day, hoping someone would talk to you about Erminia Frezzolini. But as no one did, I came. I'm family, and I don't want her memory to vanish as her talent did". He'd break my heart with the story of a young girl, tall, elegant, with long black lashes and a melancholic expression. Her capacity of singing simply, mastering long phrases, old-style potent upper register, and irreprehensible technique was exploited by practically every man she had known. Her father Giuseppe, famous bass, was also her teacher, charging her, as soon as her name rose in the sky of opera plays, three thousand francs a year. He also led the soprano to sign away all her savings before addressing her to marry Antonio Poggi although already engaged with a colleague. Poggi was a singer as well. He had paid the father forty thousand francs as a dowry, slash investment on her potential future earnings.

Erminia was one of Verdi's favorites. He had seen her at La Scala and ever since worked with her, even adapting plays to her voice and abilities.. But she was constantly guarded, isolated, and controlled by her husband. At least until, after five years of exploitation, the tenor abandoned her to marry the eccentric Giulia Samoyloff. Who eventually dumped him. At least that!

With no money of her own, Erminia had to work until elder, although her vocal talents were vanishing. Mark Twain wrote of a tragic night at the theater San Carlo in Naples. The singer would appear in the scenes, start to perform, and receive hisses and jeers from the audience. The same audience that idolatrized her only a few years before.

Poems and writings had been dedicated to her. Composers would fight for her.

While now, when she left the stage crying, she was called back in, made her start again, only to repeat the cruel fusses and derision. Again, and again.

Erminia died in Paris at 66 and alone.

Orvieto, I would conclude, is a town of storytellers, a fortress that englobes you with its folklore, mysticism, and magic. A place of tragedies that become stories. And stories that become legends. Legends to tell around a fire, to make the dark winter days a time to reflect, meditate and remember.

*In Italy, we call playing hooky, marinating the school.

LUMACHELLE ORVIETANE

Lumachelle means little snails, but we are talking of the shape, not the content. These bread rolls are super soft and gift you an explosion of cheesy flavors.
The traditional recipe calls for lard, but I prefer olive oil. If you want to try the exact recipe, simply use half the weight of lard and half of olive oil. Instead, if you want your snails a little milder in flavor, substitute Pecorino with parmesan, completely or partially.

Ingredients for ten medium/small Lumachelle:
125 gr (4.4 oz or 3/4 cup + 1 teaspoon) of 0 flour
75 gr (2.6 oz or 1/4 cup + 1 tablespoon) of lukewarm water
5 gr (0.18 oz) of fresh baker's yeast
50 gr (1.8 oz or about 1 thick slice) of Pancetta
25 gr (0.9 oz or 4 tablespoons) of grated Pecorino
25 gr (0.9 oz or 3 tablespoons) of extra virgin olive oil
salt
black pepper

Dissolve the yeast in the lukewarm water.
Place the flour on a working surface or inside the mixer bowl (kneading hook on). Form a hole in the middle and add the yeasted water. Work with your hands or the machine for a minute or so to completely incorporate the liquids. While still kneading, add a pinch of salt, a few grinds of pepper, the grated Pecorino, and the olive oil. Continue working the dough until you get a smooth and elastic result. This should take you about ten minutes with the machine and a little more by hand.
Place the dough in a bowl and cover it with a kitchen cloth, a bowl upside down, or plastic film. Place it inside the turned-off oven and let it rise for an hour.
Meanwhile, coarsely chop the Pancetta.
Take back the dough, add the Pancetta pieces, and knead with your hands to evenly distribute it. Divide the dough into ten pieces. With your hands, roll each piece to form a cylinder of about ten centimeters (four inches) in length. Roll it up from the center towards the outside to form a snail.
Line an oven sheet with parchment paper and display the Lumachelle.
Cover them with a cloth and let them rise for about twenty minutes.
Preheat the oven to 200°C/390°F.
Bake the Pancetta snails a little less than ten minutes - sorry, you'll have to monitor them - or until slightly golden on the surface.
You can serve them hot or at room temperature. You may also slice Lumachelle lengthwise and fill them with cold meats!

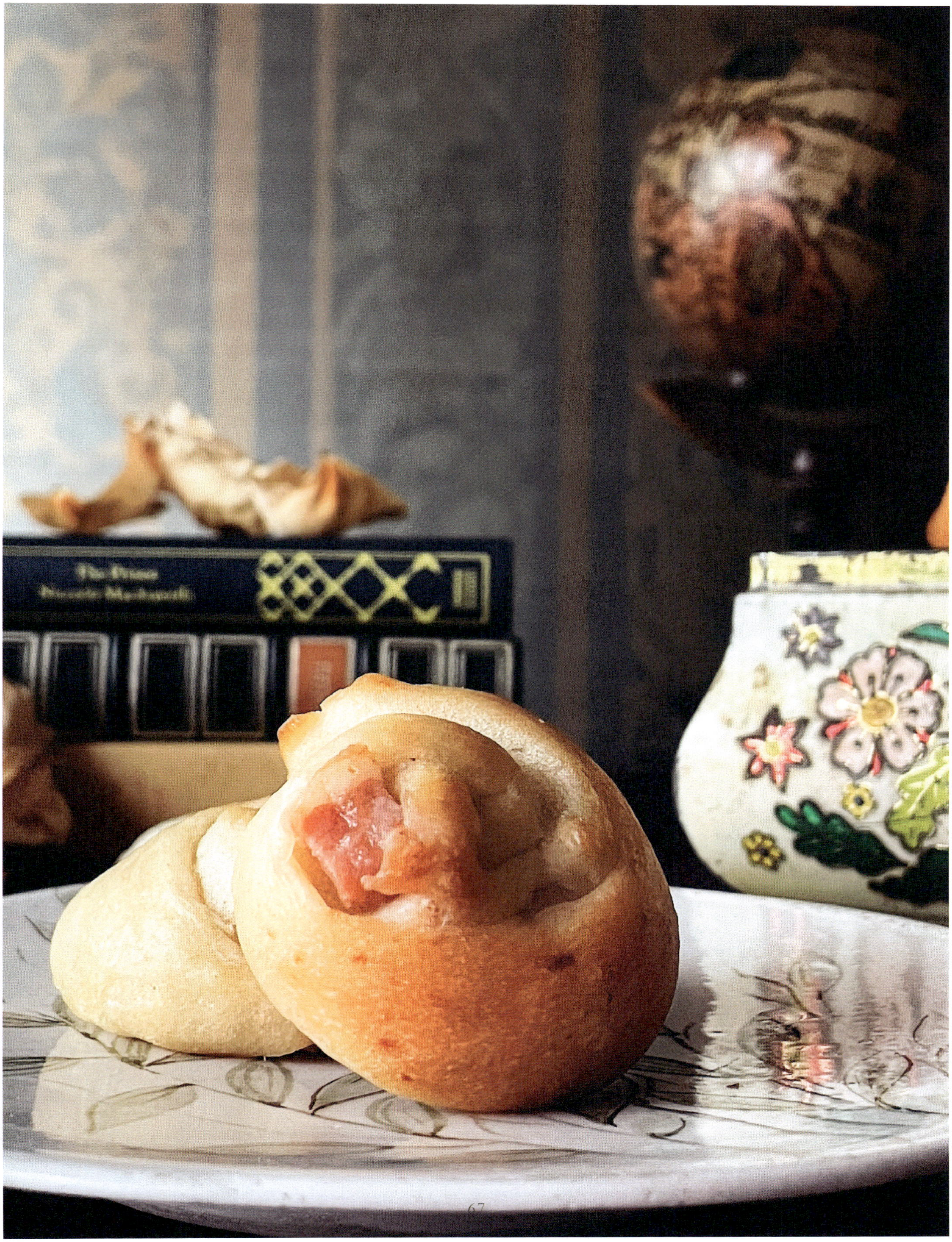

PIZZA GIALLA ORVIETANA

In Orvieto, they make a yellow pizza, which is not exactly a pizza but a savory cornflower cake. It is perfect for a charcuterie board as a tasty vehicle for all the Prosciutto, salami, and cheese delights.

Ingredients for two to four:
150 gr (5.3 oz or 1 cup + 2 tablespoons) of cornflower
1 small rosemary sprig
2-3 sage leaves
1 bay leaf
2 cloves
extra virgin olive oil
salt
black pepper
a 20 centimeters/8 inch pie pan or cake mold

Preheat the oven to 180°C/350°F.
Grease a small oven skillet, pie dish, or cake mold with a teaspoon of olive oil.
In a medium bowl, bring to a boil half a liter (two cups) of water, one teaspoon of salt, the rosemary sprig, sage leaves, bay leaf, and clove. Simmer a couple of minutes, turn off the heat and let rest for a few more minutes. Drain the liquid and discard the spices and herbs. Or simply remove them with tongs.
Return the broth to the pot and drizzle in the cornflower, a little at a time, stirring continuously. Pour in a teaspoon of olive oil and a few grinds of black pepper. Mix to incorporate.
Pour the mixture into the skillet or mold and spread evenly.
Bake the yellow pizza for thirty to forty minutes until the surface gains a golden hue. Insert a knife or skewer into the center; if it comes away clean, it's ready; if it has batter, the cake needs a few more minutes.
Once cooked, slice your yellow pizza and serve it hot or at room temperature with cold meats and cheeses!

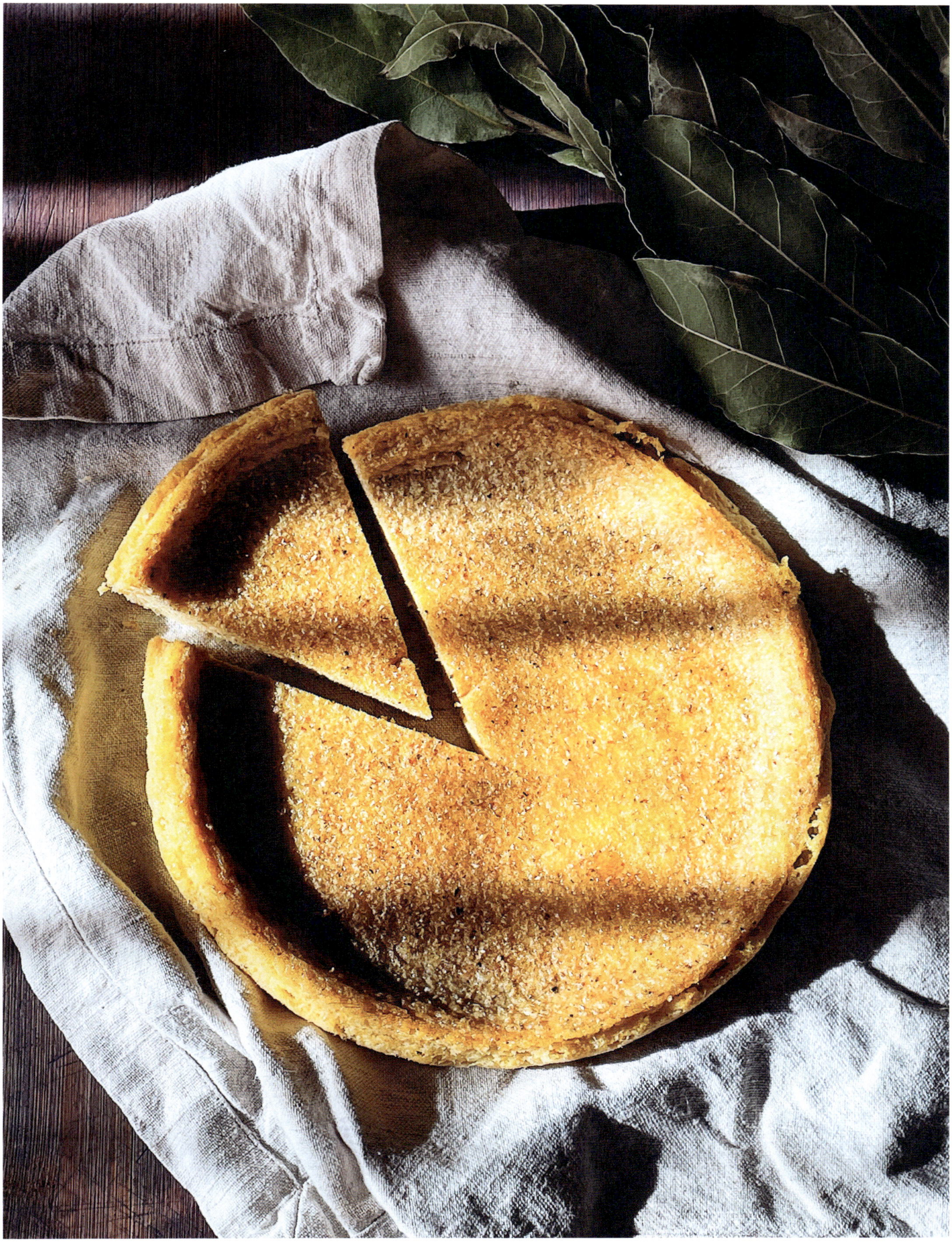

TORTA DI ORVIETO

This is Orvieto's traditional cake. A perfect breakfast cake, similar to a Bundt cake. Or a dessert, when served with Crema Pasticcera - recipe on the blog - sprinkled with candied fruit.

Ingredients for a regular cake:
400 gr (14 oz or 2 + 1/2 cup + 2 tbsp) of 00 flour + a little more for the cake mold
80 gr (2.8 oz or 1/2 cup) of raisins
14 g (0.5 oz or a little more than 1 tablespoon) of baking powder
120 gr (4.2 oz or 1/2 cup + 1 tablespoon + 1 teaspoon) of sugar
150 gr (5.3 oz) of butter at room temperature + a tablespoon or so to grease a cake mold
3 eggs
the zest of 1 lemon
salt

Place the raisins in a small cup and cover them with water.
Preheat the oven to 180°C (350 °F) - convection setting.
Grease the cake mold with the extra butter. Toss in a tablespoon or two of flour and shake the mold energetically to ensure a thin layer covers all the inside.
Sift the flour into a mixing bowl. Add the baking powder and whisk a bit. Dice the softened butter and add it to the flour. Add the sugar, the eggs, the lemon zest, and a pinch of salt. Whisk to amalgamate fully. Drain and squeeze the raisins and add them to the mixture. Stir well.
Pour the mixture into the cake mold and bake the cake for forty minutes to an hour, depending on how tall your mold is. Insert a knife or skewer into the center; if it comes away clean, it's ready; if it has batter, the cake needs a few more minutes.
Bring to room temperature, unmold the cake, and serve it.

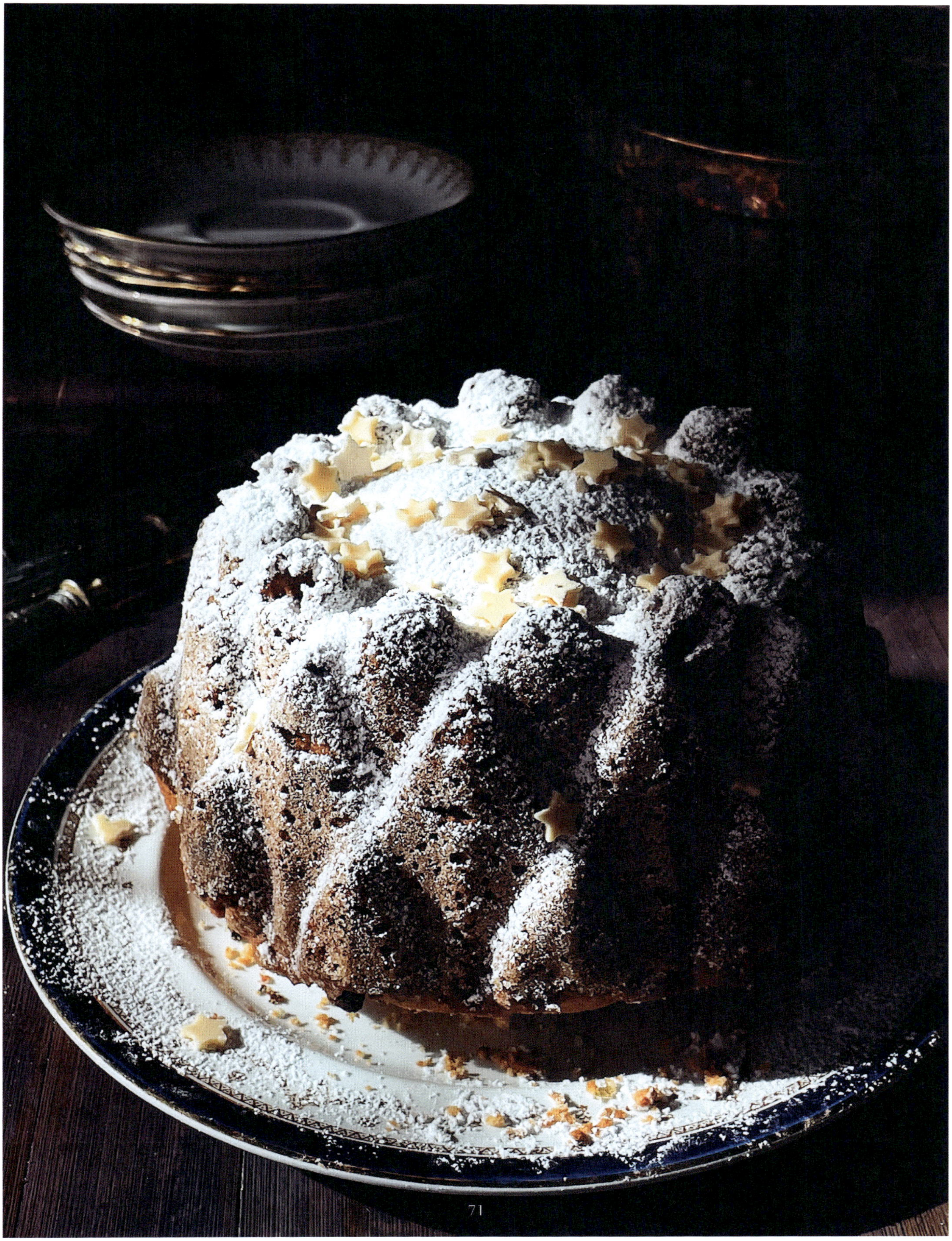

SPOLETO

If I were a hippie in the sixties, I'd drive to Umbria, rent a bike with the few pennies in my pocket, and pedal to Spoleto.

I'd find improvised accommodation. Probably a hostel, sharing the bathroom with a dozen other girls - and boys, because we love communion.

And I'd breathe art daily. I'd meet avant-garde masters of theater, ballet, visual arts, and music. I'd dance, eyes closed and swirling long skirt, in the middle of a piazza. I'd lose flowers from my hair but wouldn't care. There would be plenty in the surrounding nature to embellish me forever. I'd volunteer to clean, run around for chores and tools. I'd open and close the curtains of the stage for my new playmaker friend incessantly. I'd run to the antique shop in search of a chandelier for the Otello's scenography. I'd be invited to rehearsals and see Rudolph Nureyev pirouette. Some good soul would offer me a three hundred Lire drink at the Music and Aperitivo cafè. I'd pick a play by Mozart or Beethoven from the menu and silently sip from my glass of wine. I'd sit on the ground to listen to a poet, surrounded by eyes as dreamy as mine. Astonished at the privilege of listening to the words of Ezra Pound, Salvatore Quasimodo, and Pablo Neruda.

Timidly, I'd decant my prose with my colleagues - meaning penniless, ambitious writers. After dark, when everyone else would be asleep, smoking a cigarette under the porch of the hostel, they'd comment on my attempt to revisit the Commedia Dell'Arte, and hopefully, propose a collaboration.

Maestro Menotti, a composer from Lombardy, studied abroad, in the United States, from a very young age. Around 1956 he decided to found a festival to reunite two worlds under the sparkling, starry sky of art. The new and the old world, America and Europe. "To educate the spirit of the young". "To bring art in daily life."

He began collecting offers from anyone interested in building a bridge to bring Italy closer to the States.

Many contributed. Including a cobbler of Italian origins, who entrusted him with ten thousand dollars! And then artists, saint artists, devoted to art more than money, adhered to the project, expecting nothing but a stage. Luchino Visconti, Carla Fracci, Thomas Schippers, Tennessee Williams, Eduardo De Filippo sooner or later exposed and shared their talent with the thousands of people that came for fame, jet set, or to nourish their souls.

IN HONOREM
BEATÆ MARIÆ VIRGINIS
ANDREAS MAURUS
A FUNDAMENTIS EREXIT
ANNO DOMINI MDCCXXVI

It is fun to watch archive footage that show the perplexed faces of the locals. Their confusion when their tiny, tranquil town was filled with statues and installations. Or when in 1968, all the city monuments were wrapped as an artistic provocation. I can only imagine the suspect of some, the curiosity and enthusiasm of others. The electricity in the air. The fear of the cautious ones and the trepidation of others waiting to get electrocuted. Who would you be? Who would I be?

But Spoletini certainly weren't new to art. Teatro Caio Melisso, one of the two theaters dusted off by Menotti, was indeed founded in 1644.

By the local academy, the Accademia Degli Ottusi (obtuse). It wasn't exactly the same theater, but one built in the same place and later rebuilt.

The academy is the seventh oldest academy in Europe. Its core activities included - and still do - literary and historical studies, especially about Spoleto and poetic compositions. Their stem is a rhinoceros sharpening its horn against a rock. The motto is the Latin expression "Terendo Exacuet", to sharpen by rubbing. Sharpen ingenuity, rubbing it to free oneself from materialism and make it clear, luminous, and divine.

Beneath the early founders was a fascinating personage: Pierleone Leoni, doctor, philosopher, astronomer, and probable alchemist.

For which he was once charged, so we'll just whisper it.

He was one of the precursors of the rehabilitation of Hippocrates medicine. According to the Greek academist, our body has a natural healing force that rebalances the disharmonies caused by illness. A doctor must stimulate that energy to trigger the restorative process.

He studied and operated widely in Italy and Europe, assisting great personalities, popes, and even Lorenzo De Medici. Whom I guess he'd preferred not to.

When the Magnifico died, poisoned, Pierleone, who had aided him with anything in his power, was accused by the son Piero of being responsible - mandated by one of their enemies.

The day after the death, Pierleone was found lifeless in the well of the establishment where he stayed.

Murmurs claimed he had committed suicide drove crazy by the failure of his science/magic.

Slander, so common then, so common today.

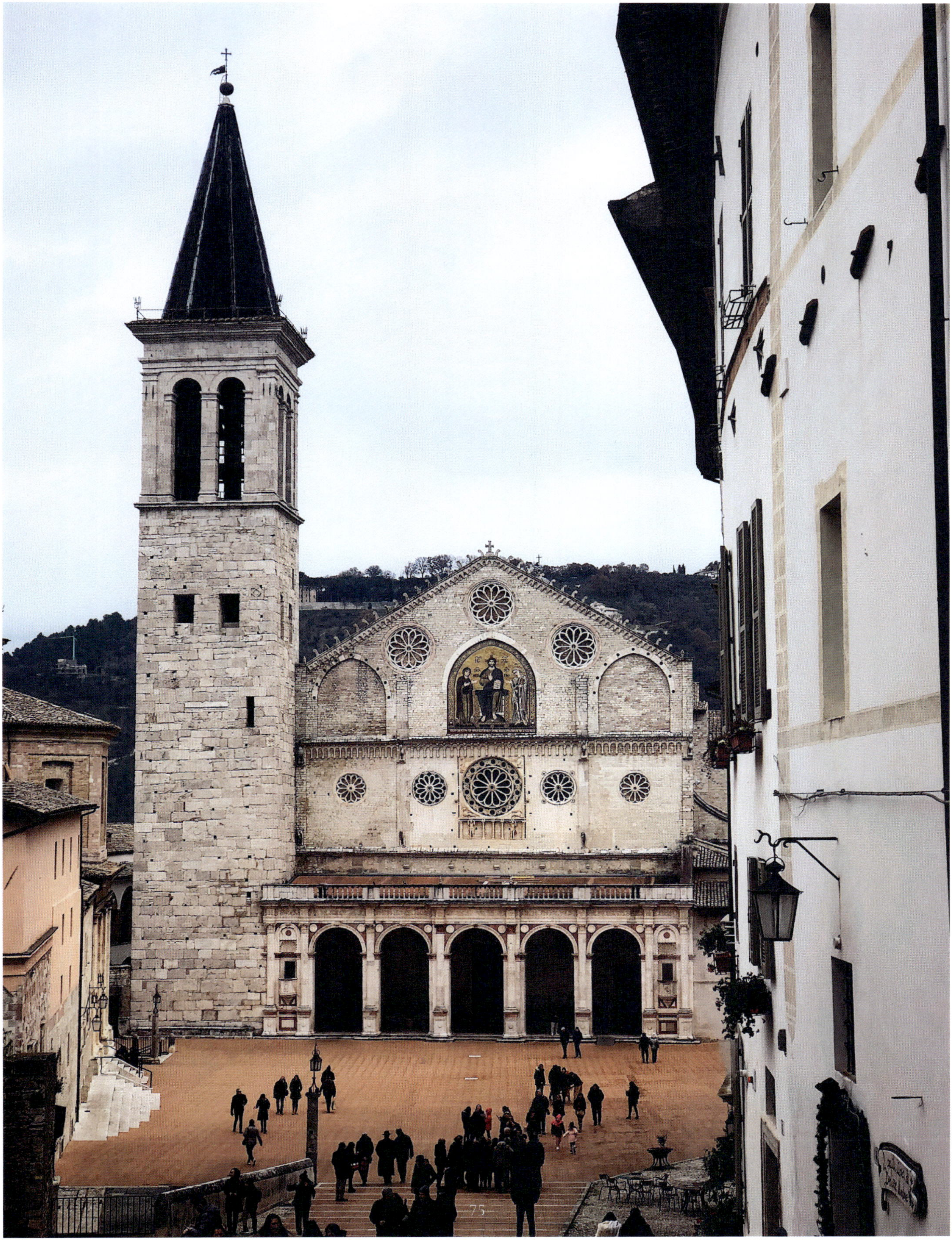

STRANGOZZI

Spoleto's Strangozzi, or Stringozzi, are very similar to fettuccine - in shape - but a little narrower and made with only flour, water, and a pinch of salt.
That's why they use semolina flour, containing much more protein.
The name refers to the Italian word "stringa", string, and was given because they recalled the leather shoelaces much more popular decades ago.

Ingredients for two:
200 gr (7 oz or about 1 cup) of semolina flour
room temperature water
1 pinch of salt

Place the flour on a working surface (for pasta, wood is better than marble), make a hole in the middle with your fist, and pour in one-quarter cup of water and a pinch of salt. Mix to incorporate, starting with your fingertips and collecting the flour on the sides. When the dough starts coming together, use your open hands to knead it by folding it over itself horizontally and pressing forward with the heel of your hand. You need an elastic and smooth dough, so this should take fifteen to twenty minutes of hand kneading.
If you are using a mixer, place the ingredients in the mixing bowl and use the kneading hook to work the dough for about ten minutes. Nevertheless, you'll need to work it a few minutes more with your hands.
Place the dough in a bowl and cover it with plastic or lay it on the working surface and cover it with a bowl, upside down, for thirty minutes.
Divide the dough into as many pieces as your servings and roll out each using a rolling pin or a pasta machine.
If you are using the rolling pin, roll each piece as thin as possible. Sprinkle the dough, the roll, and the surface abundantly with flour to make sure they don't stick together. You should form long irregular rectangles.
Lay them on a well-floured working surface. Sprinkle both sides with flour and roll them up. Cut the rolls into half a centimeter (0.2 inches) coils. Delicately unroll each coil and sprinkle with more flour to ensure they don't stick.
If you are using a pasta machine, flatten each piece of dough as much as you can with your hands and pass it through the wider setting. Repeat it once or twice. Lower the setting by one and feed the pasta through again. Repeat, lowering the setting until the penultimate (mine has nine settings, I stopped at the eighth). If, in any setting, the pasta dough breaks or gets holes, simply fold it over itself and feed it through twice. If you get rectangles too long to handle, cut them in two and proceed to feed each piece separately.
Sprinkle each side of the stretches and roll them up to cut them as described above.
Bring a big pot of salted water to a boil - about two liters (half a gallon) and one tablespoon of salt. Delicately toss in the pasta, cook it until it floats, and then two to four minutes more.
Drain and season as per your choice.

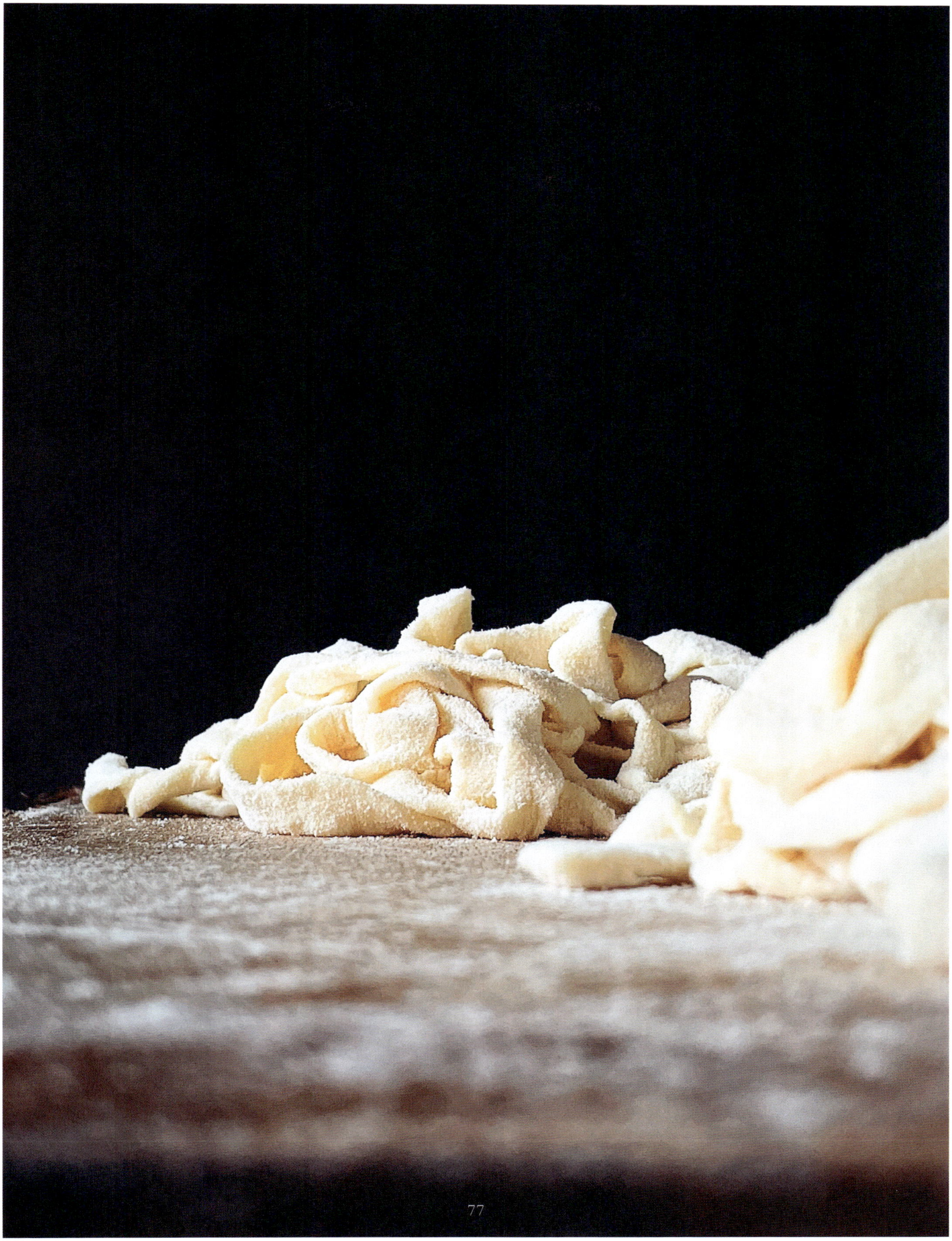

STRANGOZZI ALLA SPOLETINA

Strangozzi Alla Spoletina, the Spoleto way, is a Spring recipe. The strings are seasoned with wild asparagus that grow near the forests, between the vines, or on the hills.
To my surprise, they are cooked long and slow, which changes their flavor greatly: you'll ask yourself if you are eating asparagus or mushrooms. One thing is for sure: they taste wild!

Ingredients for two:
two servings of fresh Strangozzi
about 30 asparagus - wild if you can find them
2 heirloom or beefsteak tomatoes
1 garlic clove
1 tablespoon of finely chopped fresh parsley
sea salt
black pepper
extra virgin olive oil

With the blade of a large knife, crush the garlic clove - no need to peel it. Finely chop the parsley.
Clean the asparagus by bending each one with your hands until they split. Discard the bottom and keep the top. Slice them into tiny pieces - leave the tops a little bigger.
Cut the tomatoes into small cubes.
Heat two tablespoons of olive oil in a medium pan. Add the garlic and the parsley and brown, medium heat, until the garlic gets slightly golden - careful not to burn either - about five minutes.
Discard the garlic and add the asparagus pieces, sprinkle them with a couple pinches of salt, mix, and cook, on medium heat, until the liquids released by the vegetables dry almost completely - about five minutes. Add the tomatoes, sprinkle with another pinch of salt and a few grinds of pepper - about five -, mix, cover, lower heat to the minimum, and cook fifty minutes to an hour. Check every now and then and add a quarter cup of water, if necessary.
Bring a big pot of salted water to a boil - about two liters (half a gallon) and one tablespoon of salt. To give more flavor, you may add the discarded stems of the asparagus, tightened together with a bit of kitchen twine, so it is easily removable.
Toss in the fresh pasta and cook it until it floats and then two to four minutes more. Taste for readiness and drain it.
Season the pasta with the asparagus sauce and serve it hot, sprinkled with more fresh parsley.

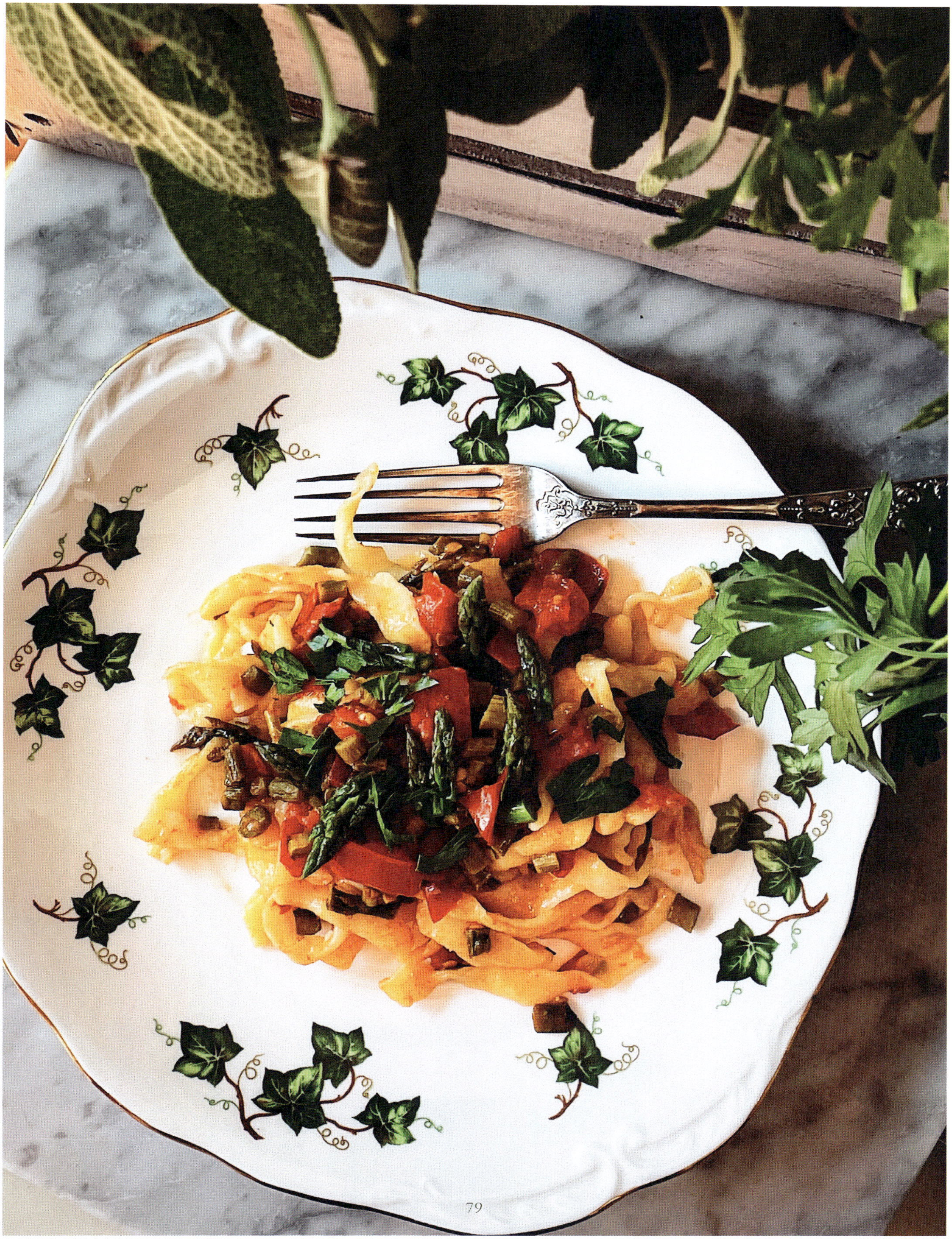

CRESCIONDA SPOLETINA

The Crescionda Spoletina is a cake with medieval origins. Indeed, the original recipe was made with lard or the grease from the chicken broth instead of olive oil. Bread instead of cookies. And with the strong opposition between Pecorino cheese, sugar, and chocolate. It was an era when culinary contrasts were way more appreciated.

It is a magical cake, in the sense that although you mix all the ingredients when cooked, three layers form: a base made of cookies and flour, a central creamy pudding layer, and a chocolaty top. It is also a typical treat for Carnival celebrations!

There's a saying, "Casa Che Vai Crescionda Che Trovi", which means that each house you visit will offer you a different Crescionda. Each family has its own unique recipe.

I was lucky to get the recipe of the hotel management school of Spoleto and started my experimentations from there.

Ingredients for a medium cake:
4 eggs
4 tablespoons of white sugar
1/2 liter (a half quart or 2 cups + 2 tablespoons) of milk
the zest of 1/2 lemon
2 tablespoons of 00 flour
100 gr (3.5 oz) of dark chocolate
100 gr (3.5 oz) of amaretti cookies
a pinch of cinnamon
2 tablespoons of Mistrà or Amaretto liquor - vodka if none of them are available
1 teaspoon of melted butter and a couple tablespoons of flour for the mold
a cake mold of about 6 inches

Separate the whites from the egg yolks.
Beat the whites - adding a pinch of salt - until firm and set them aside.
Place the yolks in a mixing bowl, add the sugar, and beat until frothy.
Crumble the amaretti cookies - you can use a food processor - and add them to the yolks.
Grate the chocolate - finely - and add it too.
Add all the other ingredients and mix well to fully incorporate.
Take back the whites and add them to the mixture delicately and with a vertical and rotatory movement. Mix until fully incorporated - don't worry if it has a bubbling appearance: it's because of the egg whites.
Grease the cake mold with the melted butter and discard the excess. Add the flour, shake well to make sure a thin patina covers the whole surface, and discard the excess.
Pour the mixture into the cake mold. Let it rest for no less than forty minutes - this will generate the stratification.
Preheat the oven to 200°C/390°F.
Bake the cake for ten minutes, then reduce temperature to 180°C/350°F. Bake thirty minutes more.
Pierce the center with a clean knife or wooden skewer; if it comes out clean, the cake is ready; if not, give it five more minutes and repeat.
Let the cake reach room temperature before slicing it! It has a pudding like consistency that needs to fully solidify.

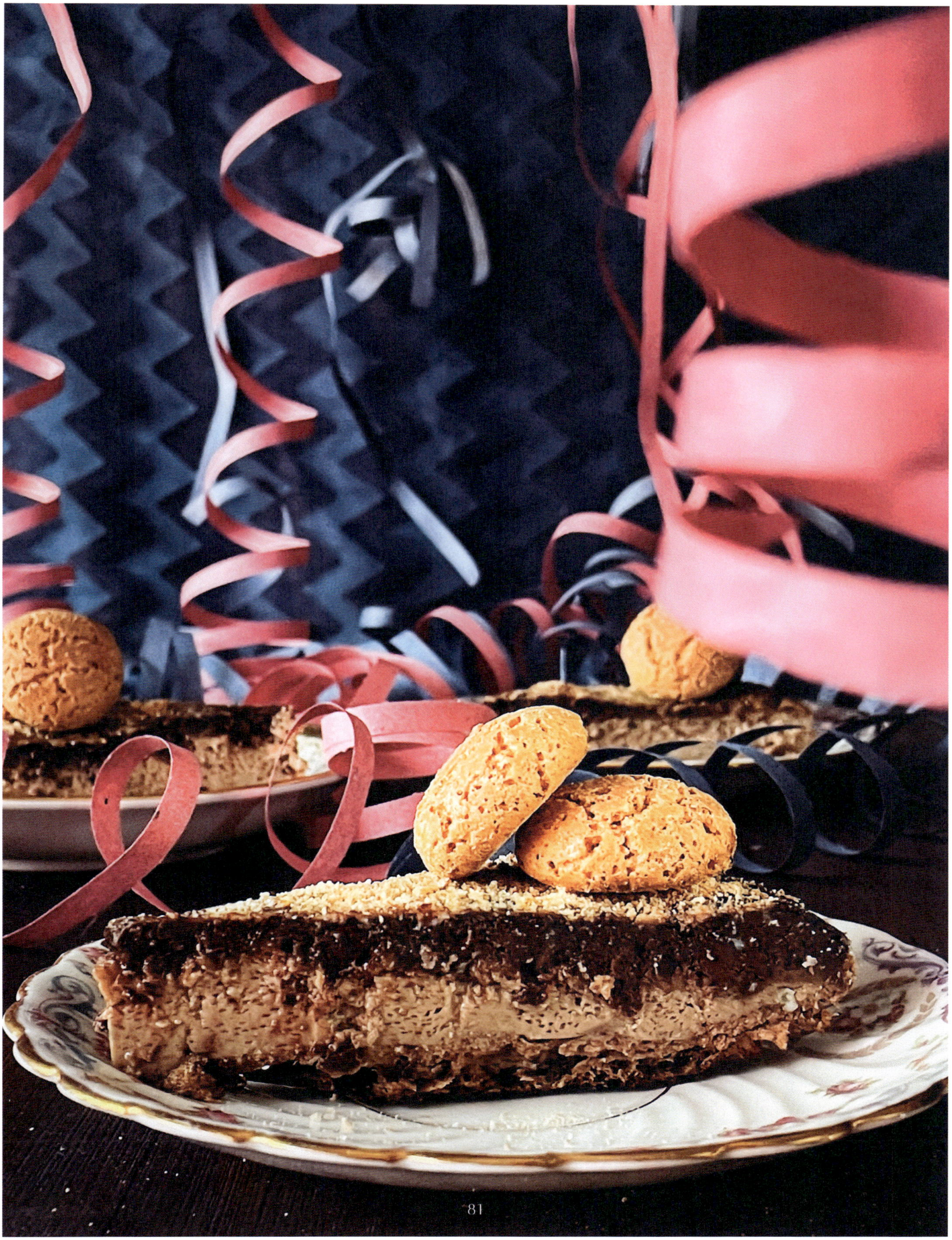

MONTEFALCO

I'm quite sure you could spend a year in the tiny town of Montefalco and never get bored. And if you do, there's plenty of wine!
You'd be engaged in preparations for this or that event. And competitions with your compaesani, townsfolks. For Easter, for example, you'd be searching the web and libraries. You'd question the elder and practice your technique in scrubbing an egg towards another to break one and leave the other intact. All this to win the Ciuccetta, or Coccetta, on Easter Monday. The competition is held in the main piazza. Anyone can participate, but let's be true, visitors and tourists have no chance to pass even the first match. There are a million things to consider, starting with choosing the right egg. You need luck. You must know your rival and fool him at Pari O Dispari* to be the one scrubbing from the top - if that's your strategy. You must research, practice, and study the story of the game. Because history - even from the fifteenth century*, always has something to teach.
Easter wouldn't be over, and your fellows would already be reminding you of your duties. Meaning your turn cleaning and brushing the ox. A beast treated way better than you ever have, even as an infant.

You'd had a remote probability of being recruited for the Summer games - relay, drumming, flag-waving, or crossbow - but you'd more likely find a place between the four hundred figurants. If you'd be keen to study, commission a tailor, and dress up as a medieval character. Besides that, you'd certainly be selected to volunteer in taking care of the ox. For the ox ride.
Depending on your accommodation, you'd be admitted to one of the color-identified teams. The red flag and knife emblem of San Bartolomeo. Maybe Sant'Agostino, with a green flag and a crowned heart. Or San Francesco, waving a blue flag with a cross. Or, lucky you, San Fortunato, the town's patron, honored with a yellow flag and a tree.
The four teams compete in an August race between their ox, led, urged, and supported by the human teams running on their side.
Fuga Del Bove is a reminiscence of a ruthless - corrida cruelty levels - folkloristic game. Centuries ago, a few days before Christmas, an ox was drunken with wine and pepper and launched through the streets of Montefalco.
A yelling and furious mob framed its run.
Bold - really? - ones waved purple scraps and rag dolls in the face of the poor, dazed, animal,

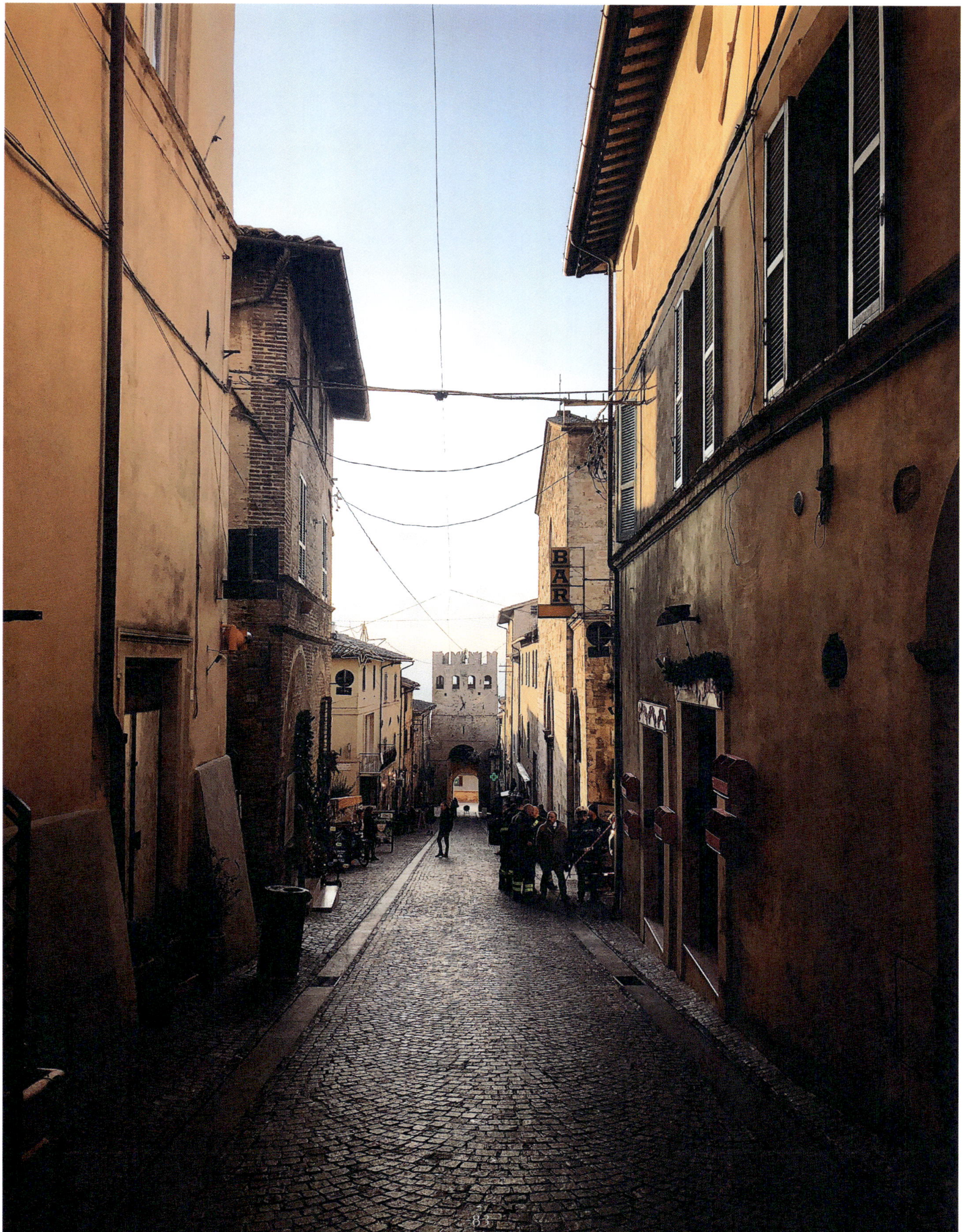
BAR

incited to vent its fury on wooden barrels. When the animal was exhausted, a pack of dogs was released to finish the poor creature's life. The meat was then distributed to every family and cooked for the Christmas lunch as an auspicious ritual. And we say intensive farming is cruel. Of course, it is, but at least nowadays, in many places, humans are atoning for the sins of their ancestors. If that's of any help. Some are vegetarian; some are vegan. But I doubt there are many in Montefalco, especially on the day of the Fuga Del Bove. After the run, everyone rushes to the historic taverns named after the saints and teams. In each, wine flows steady and traditional plates are served. The green one specializes in the Egg Stracciata: a runny scrambled egg dusted with black truffle. The red offers the Rocciata, strudel, and goose gnocchi. The blue one makes the best Pere Al Sagrantino - pears cooked in Sagrantino wine - and Tozzetti. The lucky yellow instead triumphs in making Gnocchi Ai Quattro Formaggi: four-cheeses gnocchi.

Soon after the ox celebrations, it is time to prepare the Festa Della Vendemmia, the harvesting feast. This time you might be selected for more artistic duties, like decorating the floats. While Stornelli (folk songs) bands play, an allegorical cart from each district of Montefalco parades in the main piazza. The carts are themed after harvesting and represent a custom or tradition related to this time of the year. After the show, the same costumed, happy, and maybe a bit tipsy humans share with the audience wine and local products: Prosciutto, salami, savory tarts, even pasta dishes.

During the remaining months, you'd have plenty of time to visit the many churches and palaces, and learn about the local legends. Including the one about the Beato Pellegrino. A Spanish pilgrim visiting Montefalco to pray Santa Chiara and then Sant'Agostino. The man fell asleep in the church and was found the next day, still bent on praying. When the priest got closer, though, he realized the man was dead. The city took care of his funeral and burial. But the next day, the pilgrim was found, again, bent on praying. So, for a couple more times, until the congregation decided to transfer him to the bell tower. After one hundred years, the body, that didn't smell nor decompose, was secured in a theca inside the church. It is still there. And voilà! I found you a Halloween activity too.

*Pari o Dispari is a finger counting game. Two players throw numbers, which are summed. The winner is the player that chose even or odd.

**The Ciuccetta or Coccetta was, apparently, introduced to Montefalco by soldiers accompanying the king of Hungary, Mattia Corvino, residing in situ for a while.

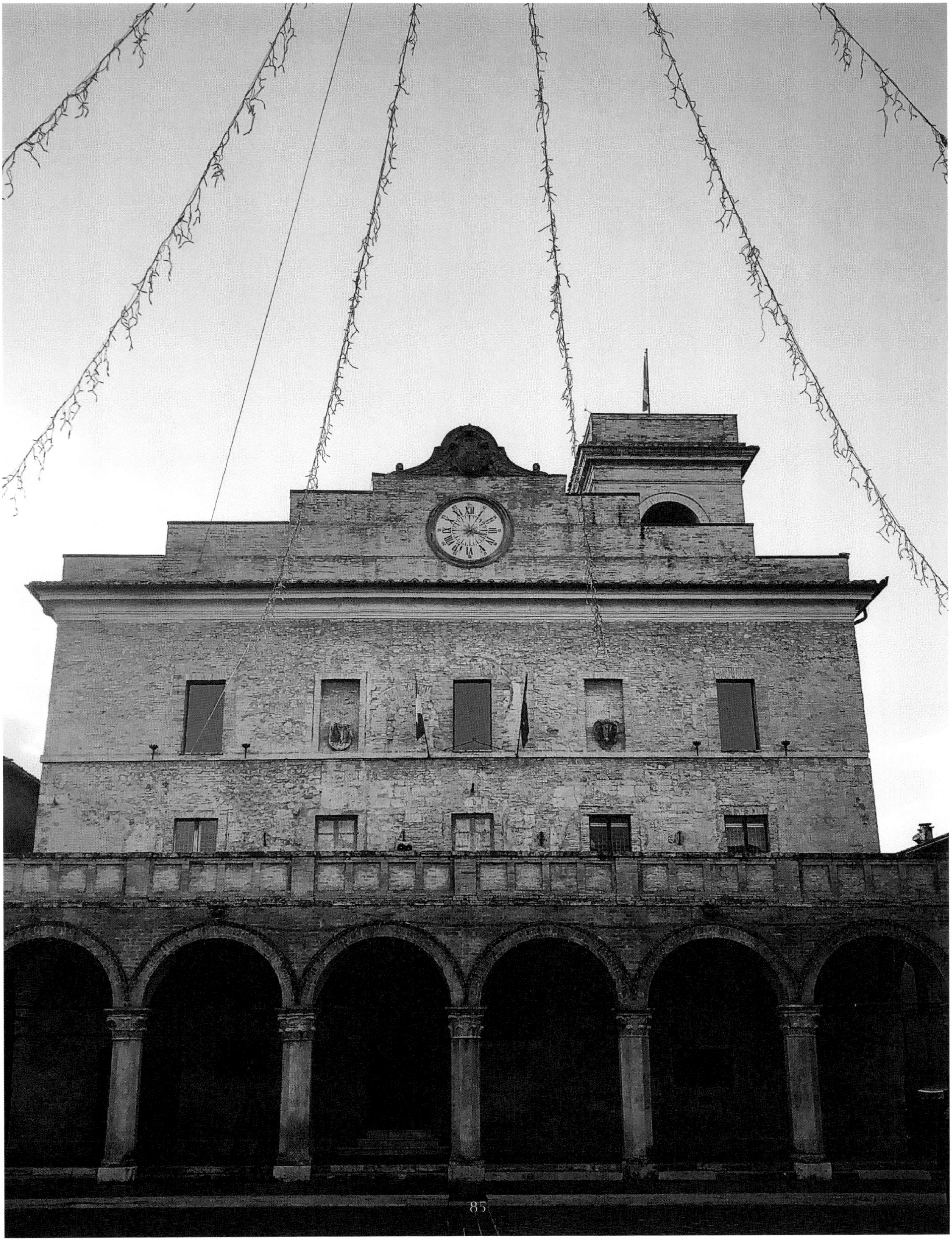

WINES OF UMBRIA

Montefalco is also the destination for pilgrims of another nature: wine lovers. Sagrantino and Sagrantino Passito are the local holy grails. The first is a highly tannic, palate-drying wine perfect to pair greasy and juicy eternally simmered meats. The second, instead, is an ideal companion for chocolate cakes.

I have a proposal for you - I'll be doing the same -: a Wine Club. For each of these wines, we'll prepare a special night. Find the wine, of course, and taste it with the recommended pairings.

Here's a short and sweet I.D. for each of the wines produced in the places we are visiting here. An Umbrian feast!

SAGRANTINO

Made in: Montefalco, mostly.

Made with: 100% Sagrantino grapes.

Color: intense ruby red, brownish when aged. Almost impenetrable to light.

Aroma: violet, sour cherry, blackberry, blueberry, dried flowers, plum, star anise. Tobacco leaves, wood, cocoa, and even menthol when aging.

Texture: full-bodied, warm.

Taste: very, very tannic, astringent - so much some interpret it as a fault.

Aging: at least thirty-three months and up to twenty years.

Curiosities: besides Umbria, there's a tiny production of Sagrantino in California and Australia.

Sagrantino, once, was called Sacrantino, assonance with the Italian word sacro, sacred. It was offered during functions and drank on Easter, paired with the traditional roasted lamb. But Sagrantino had almost disappeared in the early twentieth century. Luckily the Caprai family, in the seventies and collaborating with the University of Milan, decided it was time to reclaim the past and proudly produce unicity!

Pairings: Let's taste it with a Brasato or simply with thirty-six months aged Parmigiano.

SAGRANTINO PASSITO

Made in: Montefalco.

Made with: 100% Sagrantino grapes, withered on wooden mats for a year.

Color: intense ruby tending towards garnet.

Aroma: blackberry and blueberry jam.

Taste: sweet and slightly tannic.

Aging: at least four months.

Curiosities: until the seventies, Sagrantino was only Passito. It was with the revival of this and other local varieties that the dry version came alongside.

To date, it appears that the vine was introduced to the region between the fourteenth and fifteenth centuries by Franciscan Friars. The grapevines were first cultivated inside the city walls and severely governed.

Pairings: Let's try it with a creamy chocolate cake, or, as suggested by Clara Di Bonaventura of thewinesalad.com, with a Sacher Torte!

MONTEFALCO ROSSO

Made in: Montefalco.

Made with: Sangiovese, Sagrantino, other vines for no more than 30%.

Color: ruby red with purplish hues.

Aroma: blackberry jam, cherries, sour cherries, and wild cherries - withered. Tobacco and vanilla are developed when aging.

Texture: full-bodied.

Taste: smooth and warm, but even fresh.

Aging: at least eighteen months.

Pairings: Let's taste it with a simple, medium or rare, grilled steak!

ORVIETO DOC

Made in: Orvieto and a small quantity in the bordering Lazio.

Made with: Procanico or Grechetto minimum 60%.

Color: pale yellow.

Aroma: peaches in syrup, honey, raisins, hazelnuts.

Texture: dry and soft.

Taste: sapid and mineral because of the tuff ground.

Curiosities: Gabriele D'Annunzio defined it as "the sun of Italy in a bottle".

Etruscans already cultivated and dedicated themselves to the art of vinification between the 8th and 3rd century B.C. They carved out caves from the volcanic soil to use as cellars.

Orvieto DOC was called the popes' wine because of their preference both for the site and the wine production.

Luca Signorelli, who painted the Last Judgment frescoes in the Cathedral of Orvieto, included one thousand liters of Orvieto wine in his compensation - per year!

You may find four classifications: Orvieto DOC, Orvieto Classico DOC - from vines in the original production area, Orvieto Superiore DOC, superior quality; Orvieto Classico Superiore DOC, la creme de la creme. Plus sweet and semi-sweet versions: Dolce and Abboccato.

Pairings: Let's try it with Pasta Alle Vongole, Pizza with grilled veggies, or truffle dusted eggs.

ORVIETO MUFFA NOBILE

Made in: Orvieto.

Made with: Procanico or Grechetto minimum 60%.

Color: gold yellow, amber when aging.

Aroma: caramelized fruit, honey-covered flowers, nuts, candied citrus zest

Texture: velvety.

Taste: sweet with a sapid and acid hue and medicinal herbs aftertaste.

Pairings: Let's taste it with a plain cheesecake. Or with foie gras, Gorgonzola, Stilton, or aged Cheddar.

TREBBIANO SPOLETINO

Made in: Spoleto.

Made with: 100% Trebbiano Spoletino

Color: deep yellow, very transparent, delicate green hues.

Aroma: yellow fruits - even tropical fruits -, wet stone, and flintstone when aging.

Taste: fresh and acid, mineral aftertaste. Aromatic herbs and citrus.

Texture: quite consistent.

Curiosities: It is one of the most ancient vines in Umbria.

Trebbiano Spoletino was abandoned in the sixties. Corporations had imposed international varieties to penetrate the market and homologate the product. Luckily, it's back!

Pairings: Let's try it with sashimi or Mozzarella Di Bufala. Or even the simplest Pasta Burro e Salvia - with butter and sage.

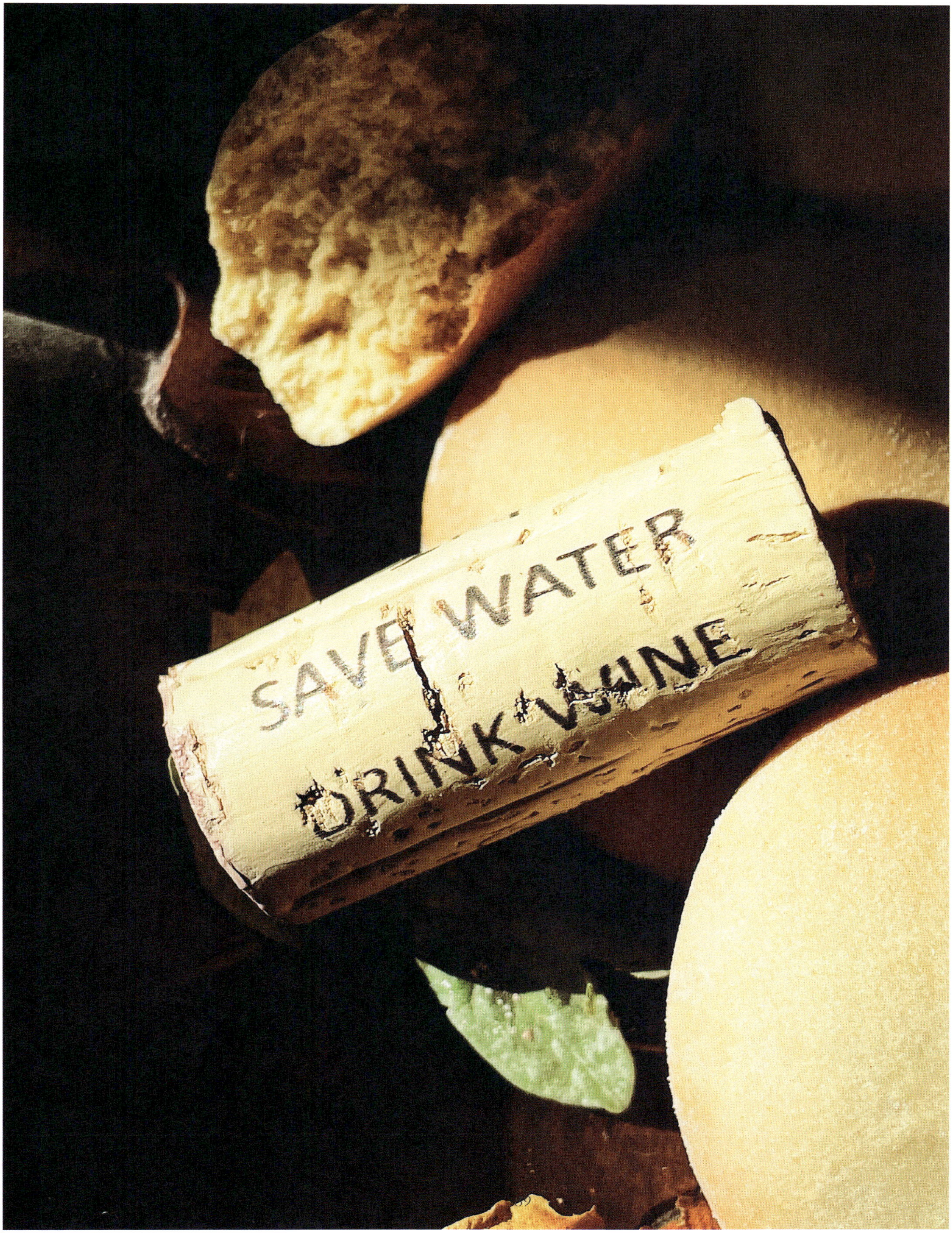
SAVE WATER
DRINK WINE

GNOCCHI AL SAGRANTINO PASSITO

When I told my vintner I was making gnocchi with Sagrantino Passito he was enthusiastic. He told me he had heard of many other wines used to make gnocchi but never Sagrantino Passito. I still have to pass by to relate the wonderful aroma and creamy and easy condiment!

Ingredients for two:
500 gr (18 oz) of floury potatoes
about 150 gr (5.3 oz or or 3/4 cup + 2 tablespoons + 2 teaspoons) of 00 flour - probably more
1/2 beaten egg
1/2 cup of Sagrantino Passito
salt

for the seasoning:
1/2 cup of Sagrantino Passito
2 tablespoons of butter
2 tablespoons of grated aged Pecorino cheese

Peel the potatoes, dice them into medium/small chunks, and steam them for about fifteen minutes, or until fork tender. Still hot, mash them with a potato ricer or masher. Spread them evenly over a floured surface to let steam out. Once there's no more steam, add the beaten egg and the wine, and mix with a spoon. Start adding the flour while also working the dough gently and the minimum necessary. With a spoon first and then with your hands. It doesn't have to be elastic: stop adding flour once it is workable, and you can form cylinders. If you added too much flour, work the dough with wet hands until it is malleable.
Form two and a half centimeters/one-inch large cylinders by rolling a piece of dough at a time.
With a cutter or a knife, cut the cylinders into two and a half centimeters/one-inch pieces. Display the gnocchi over parchment paper or on a floured surface, one layer and spaced to avoid sticking. Sprinkle them with a little flour.
Bring a big pot of salted water to a boil - about two liters (half a gallon) and two tablespoons of salt - there's no salt in the gnocchi.
Meanwhile, melt the butter in a small pan over low heat, add the Sagrantino wine, mix and bring to a boil. Turn off the heat.
Gently transfer the gnocchi and cook them until they float.
Drain them and season them with the Sagrantino sauce, then sprinkle them with Pecorino cheese. Devour while still hot!

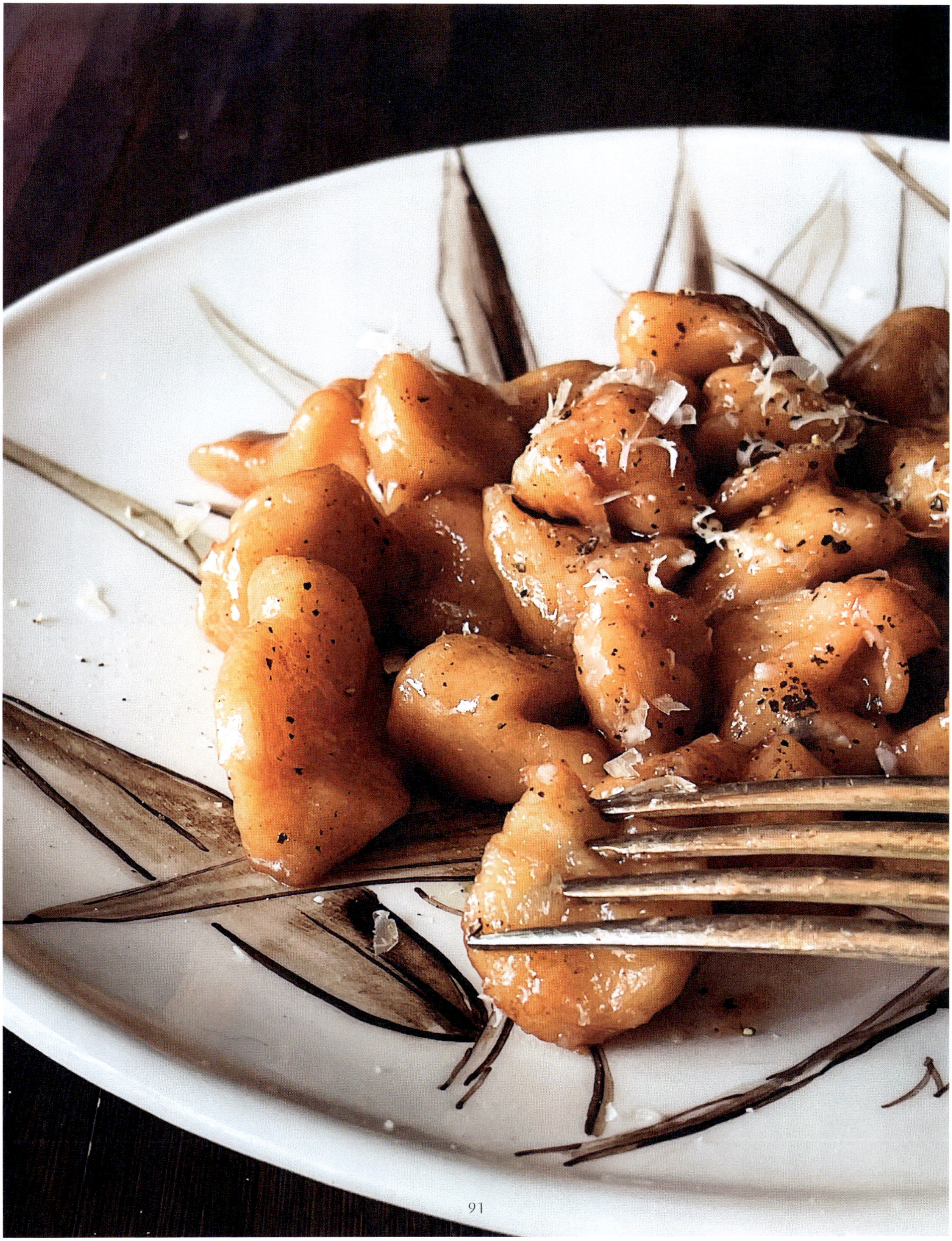

TOZZETTI

As mentioned earlier, Tozzetti, although traditional to the whole Umbria region, are savored in Montefalco on the night after the ox run. Dipped in Sagrantino Passito as a dessert. Just like Tuscan neighbors do with Cantucci in Vinsanto. Indeed, the recipes are very similar: a bread like loaf baked, sliced, and baked again. The truth is there are innumerable recipes in both areas and wonderful variations to try: chocolate chips, pistachios, dried fruits... This is an almost plain recipe, a base to start your experimentations.

Ingredients for about a dozen cookies:
200 gr (7 oz or 1 + 1/2 cups) of 0 flour
1 egg
2 teaspoons of baking powder
100 gr (3.5 oz or 1/2 cup) of sugar
100 gr (3.5 oz) of butter
20 gr (0.7 oz or 2 tablespoons) of raisins
50 gr (1.8 oz or 1/4 cup + 1 tbsp) of peeled hazelnuts
50 gr (1.8 oz or 1/4 cup + 1 tbsp) of peeled almonds
1 pinch of cinnamon

Preheat the oven to 180°C/350°F - convection setting.
Place the raisins in a small bowl or cup and cover them with water.
In a mixing bowl, beat the egg with the sugar until frothy. Dust in the flour, cinnamon, and baking powder. Mix well. Incorporate the softened and roughly diced butter working the dough with the mixer - kneading hook on - or with your hands. You are looking for a bread like consistency.
Squeeze the raisins well, then scatter a tablespoon of flour over them and shake the bowl for a thin film to cover them. This will help them distribute evenly and adhere without falling on the bottom during baking.
Toss the nuts and raisins inside the mixing bowl and knead the dough to amalgamate.
With your hands, form an oblong loaf, about twenty centimeters/eight inches long and four centimeters/one and a half inch tall.
Line an oven sheet with parchment paper and lay the loaf on top. Bake the loaf for twenty minutes.
Take it out of the oven and let the temperature decrease until manageable.
With a large knife, cut the loaf into one and a half centimeters/half-inch slices.
Display them back on the oven sheet and toast them in the oven - same temperature - for ten to fifteen minutes or until lightly toasted.
Bring the Tozzetti to room temperature and store them in a jar for up to a week or two.

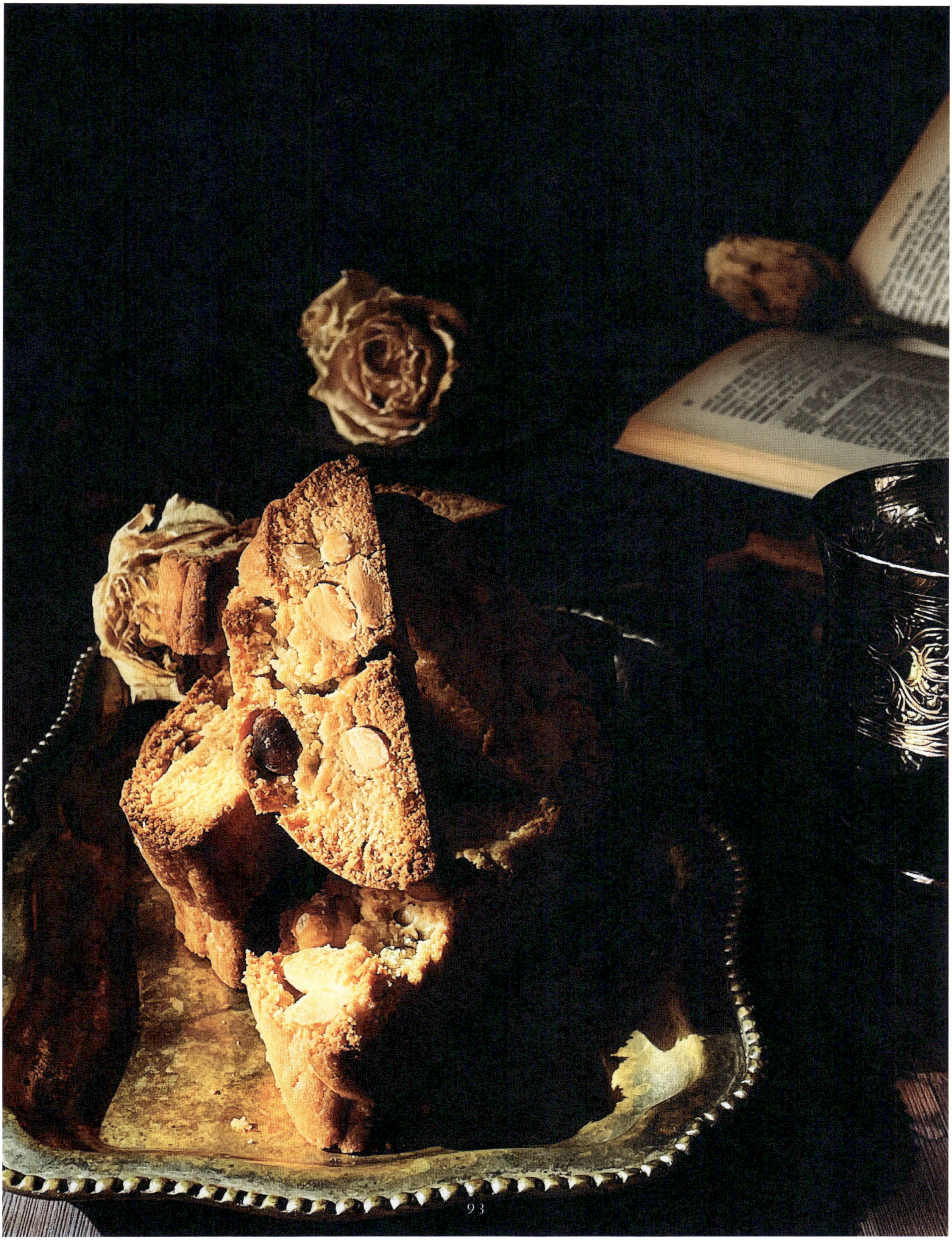

ATTORTA

The Attorta, elsewhere named Rocciata, is, obviously, the result of the many dominations and contaminations of Umbria. It is a strudel shelled in an olive oil instead of butter - thus crunchier - dough. Lastly sprinkled, upon out of the oven with Alchermes. and sugar.

Ingredients for a medium cake:
100 gr (3.5 oz or 1/2 cup + 2 tablespoons) of 00 flour
1/4 cup of white wine + a few tablespoons to soak the raisins
1 tablespoon of extra virgin olive oil
2 teaspoons of sugar
1 pinch of salt
a pinch or two of cinnamon

for the filling:
400 gr (14 oz, about one and a half) of apples
40 gr (1.4 oz, about 10-15) of walnuts
1 tablespoon of raisins
1 teaspoon of cocoa - optional
2 teaspoons of sugar + 1 more for garnishing
2 teaspoons of extra virgin olive oil
a few pinches of cinnamon
1/4 cup of Alkermes liquor

Place the raisins in a small cup and cover them with a couple of tablespoons of wine.
If necessary, crack the walnuts. Coarsely chop them - the work of a big knife is enough.
Peel and slice - thin but not transparent - the apples. Place them in a bowl and add the walnuts, cocoa powder, sugar, olive oil, and cinnamon. Squeeze the raisins, discard the wine, and toss them in the bowl. Mix well with your hands or a spoon. Set aside.
Preheat the oven to 180°C/350°F.
Place the flour in a bowl or the mixer's bowl and pour in the wine, olive oil, sugar, salt, and cinnamon. Mix and then knead until a ball of smooth and elastic dough forms (around the kneading hook if you are using a mixer).
On a working surface - lightly dusted with flour - roll out the dough to form a rectangle the size - more or less - of a letter paper. Roll the rectangle around the pin and transfer it over a piece of parchment paper or a clean kitchen cloth. Scatter the apple and nuts filling evenly through the dough but stop about four centimeters/one and a half inch before the perimeter.
Helping yourself with the cloth or parchment paper, roll the dough over itself, very delicately as it might break.
Seal the edges of the roll, bending them and pressing them between your fingers.
Always delicately and helping yourself with the cloth or paper, transfer the roll to an oven sheet lined with parchment paper - or simply use the one you already have. You can give the roll a snake-like shape, twisting it, or a horseshoe shape.
Bake the Attorta for thirty to forty minutes - until the surface goldens.
Right out of the oven, sprinkle the Arkermes over the surface with the help of a spoon or brush. And dust it with the extra sugar.
Done! Let the temperature decrease a bit before serving.

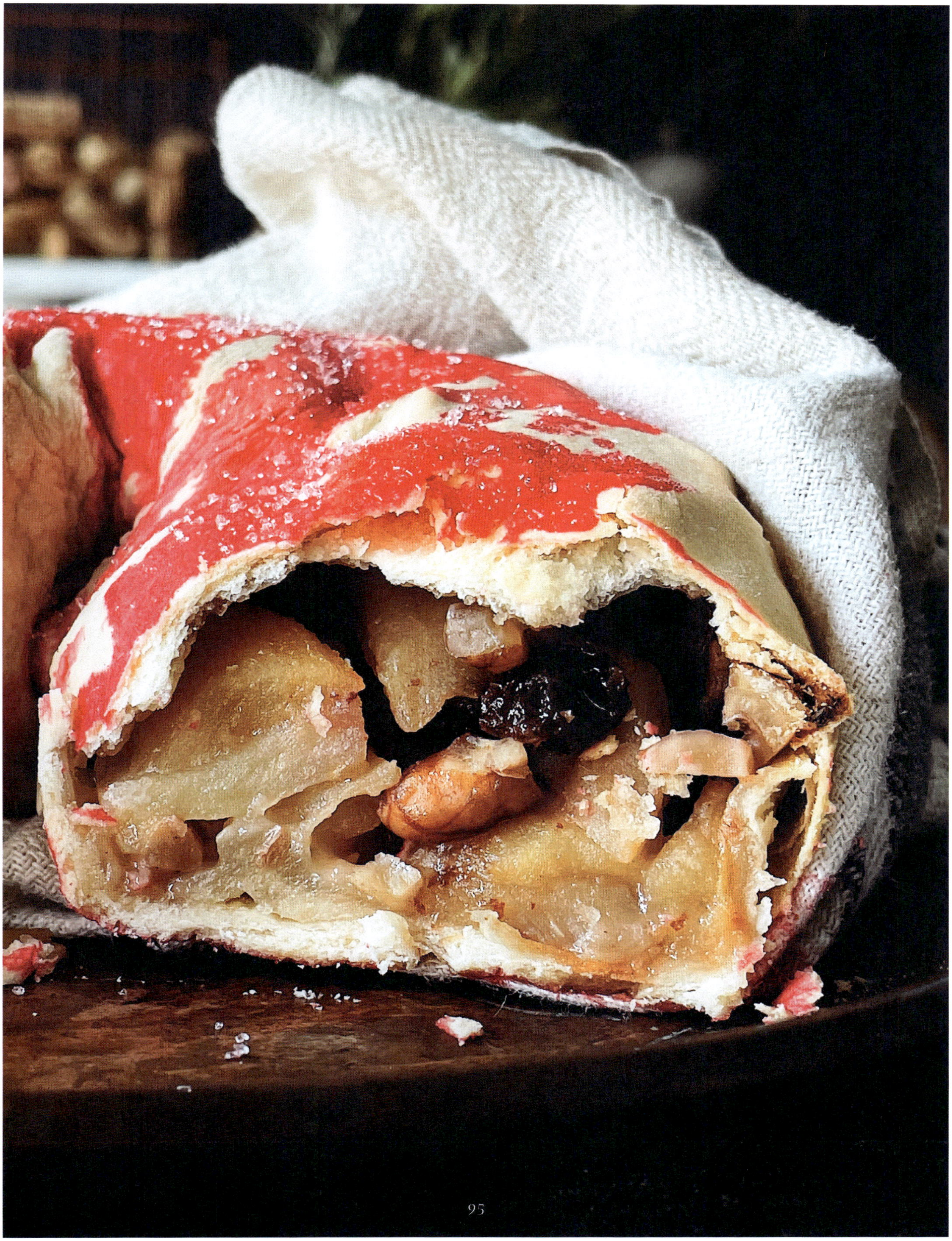

NORCIA

The most illustrious citizen of Norcia is San Benedetto, the founder of the Regola Benedettina. A lifestyle guide for monks and nuns: Ora et Labora et Lege. Pray and Work and Read. Those "et" and "and" are important.

San Benedetto was born around 480 A.D. in Norcia, twin brother to another saint, Santa Scolastica. At a very young age, they were sent by their wealthy father to Rome to finish their studies. Both were surprised to find the city dissolute and corrupted above any imagination. Benedetto, first, left the city and embraced a hermit life in a grotto in the town of Subiaco - an hour drive from Rome. The more he isolated, the more consent and disciples he gained: the recurring scheme for the birth of many monasteries. In thirty years, Benedetto founded about thirteen monasteries, all under his spiritual guidance. Then, he decided to build yet another one for himself in Cassino, another couple of hours drive. During his peaceful, although less solitary, life there, Benedetto wrote the Regola: a manuscript dictating the rules of behavior for a monastery. It wasn't the first Regola. Indeed, hermits, monasteries, and rules were concepts arriving from the East many years earlier than his birth.

Still, La Regola spread in all of Europe. Years later, Carlo Magno and his son Ludovico Il Pio even imposed it as the primary rule for every monastery in the old world. The sociological reason is simple. Benedetto's rule was milder than the others. And it comprised most of the pleasures of life. Although a simple and rural life. Still today, an Italian expression is "Quello Che Passa Il Convento," literally translated into "what the convent passes". It is used when you are asking someone to settle with what is feasible - because of lack of money, time, or energy! Most of the monks came from noble and wealthy families. We are talking of a time in which kings and rulers imposed their designated abbeys, some even laic. They might have been their sons or daughters (abbesses), relatives, or people claiming their favors. Because much money and power were involved. Taxes and fines were collected by the monasteries in return for prayers. Plus, for every sin, contributions were added. Twenty-four hours, seven days a week, an incessant lament came from behind the walls of the convents: anyone paying could claim his salvation through prayers. The praying friars and nuns were acculturated and, although not having much choice - they were sent at a very young age to pray for their relatives -,

97

still with a voice in society and a little power in the community. So, it appears credible that many endorsed this milder rule. If you consider the alternatives - wars, crusades, marrying and being subdued by a stranger - the Rule sounded like a much better, even pleasant way of spending your days. It included cultural activities - Legere! - and a lifestyle that was at least acceptable. Each monk was entitled to four hundred fifty grams (one pound) of bread per day. Two cooked meals, plus vegetables and legumes. White meat and an abundant glass of wine. Red meat was permitted only to the ill and weak. Wake up was later in the winter and anyway later than in other monasteries.

"Everything in moderation" could've been the Regola's mantra. Although it makes me smile that my friends and I, and many Italians, identify San Benedetto's hometown, Norcia, as the place for gargantuan meals and only-this-time immoderate boozing.

Anyway, many, still nowadays, consider La Regola a guide to a more spiritual, complete, and interesting life. Father Natale Brescianini, life coach and training consultant, has a clear opinion over the enormous opportunities companies and workers have in implementing it. His words, I must admit, resonated with me much more than I would ever expect, being it a religious source.

Ora, pray, is the starting point. When I read the Regola, I was impressed with this prescription. It implied a concept I have rediscovered with time: silence, too often underrated.

Silence to listen, silence after posing questions - to oneself and to others. Silence even when the answer is not immediate. And instead of a hasty, made-up answer. And, even more important, the will to formulate those questions. To doubt the way things are, the way we act, the way we think, our value system. "The most dangerous phrase in the language is 'we've always done it this way'" is a quote attributed to Grace Hopper, an American computer scientist and United States Navy's rear admiral. Ora is the research within our souls. A new, evolving spiritualism. When I read other parts of the Regola, I felt a bit anxious. There were a lot of mentions of a vindictive god, a lot of bossing over every minute aspect of one's life, plus tragic consequences for one's misbehavior. What about free will, personality, and making mistakes to learn the lesson and evolve?

It also proclaimed: "laziness is the enemy of the soul." But we have great thinkers promoting creative idleness! And millions of people rediscovering our Italian Dolce Far Niente! Then I heard father Natale's analysis, and everything fell into place. Or most of it. I'll probably end up making my own rule. Which is his recommendation anyway.

Labora, work. Sacred work. The work that ennobles men, according to Darwin. We've lost this concept, or at least many of us have; we feel more and more like slaves, missing out an hour of life for every minute spent in the office or at the PC. Underpaid, and underestimated. Captivated by policies and

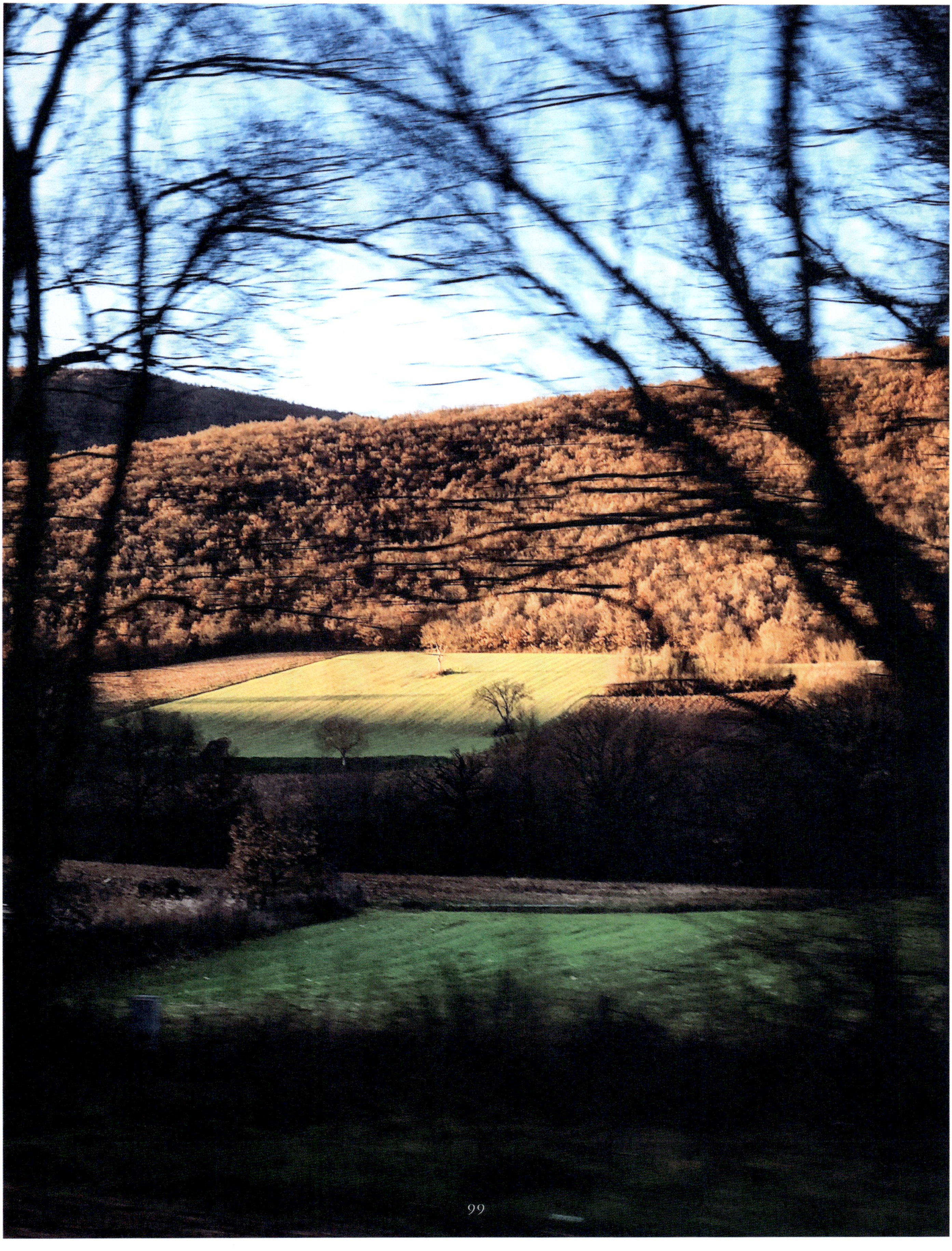

procedures.

What's the point? All those who settled for the basic income declining any job offer that wouldn't at least double it must have questioned. The point is - let the one who left a "good" job for an adventure tell you - that you can't let your brain atrophy. It would be a true, unforgivable sin. You need to nourish it with challenges, with problems to solve, with the excitement of the unknown. You need to build something if you want to honor your humanity. I'm not talking of money, beware; I'm talking of doing something with your gifts. No matter your age, position, or condition. I'm talking of re-drawing work as an opportunity to give meaning to our existence. Men and women at the center of their life through the creation of something. If it is not a masterpiece - I'd love to be Da Vinci, but I'm not - it can be a fabulous answer to an email. It can be a suggestion to better a product. Mindful motherhood. Changing the destiny of an alumni. Spreading smiles into the world.

Monks' primary occupations were sublime: creating book covers from animal skins. Producing oak gall or carbon and acacia gum ink. Both, to create majestic manuscripts: bibles, saint biographies, historical chronicles, or copies of the classics. But San Benedetto asked them to fulfill also grunt tasks: cooking, cleaning, and gardening. Humility to ground them. To find significance even in the smallest, apparently insignificant, task. Mainstream has convinced us that only appearing fabulous on a cover of a magazine is special. Or having one million followers on social media. That if we don't gain either of them, we should give up any aim to being special. But people are special! Every person that gives a purpose - or many purposes - to their life is exceptional. Each time we enrich ourselves or others, with even the tiniest detail. Each time we are building a little piece of a better world. Each time we add a little something to the slightest gesture, we are ultra-mega super special! Just not touted, which makes it even more extraordinary.

Legere, read, has a wide significance. For monks, it was sacred texts or personal lectures. For us, it is an extensive range of choices. Learn new things. Update our knowledge. Nourish our inner life with culture: art galleries, movies, courses. But also, a conversation about a topic we know or don't.

As you can see, all three precepts are intercorrelated. One feeds the other. One makes questions another may answer. One incites the rise of even more questions. That's why there's an "et" after each. But those conjunctions also mean we must find our personal balance between them. How much of each depends on our personality and preferences but also on the specific moment we are living. More Ora or more Labora? Lege in the morning or in the evening? Only you can answer.

It's the new humanism, dear friends, a time to put us at the center of everything once again. To legitimate our spirituality, our choices, and our being.

A

Marco

"Boutique del Pecoraro"

MARJORAM OIL

I found this recipe in my book about Monastery-made remedies, La Farmacia Di Dio. It has become a great companion in researching natural cures and ancient knowledge. I also went a little deeper researching marjoram's story and, my great passion, floriography meanings.
For ancient Greek and Romans, the plant symbolized joy and happiness. And it still does, in a sweeter way. The language of flowers attributes to it the meaning of generosity and comfort. A perfect addition to a bouquet for a parent. A good one! In the 1800s, marjoram gained an additional meaning: countryside pleasures. So, I guess it would be perfect on an invitation for a picnic! Somehow related is another symbology: the contemplative man. Marjoram roots don't ground too deep, just the necessary. Like the man who needs to have his feet in the ground but also to protrude towards the higher spiritual world.
In terms of householding, the plant's leaves are great for polishing wood furniture and pavements. I tried, and it actually works. But I would confine it to dark wood. My light cutting board gained a - just hinted - green hue. The perfume, though, was delightful.
Flowers instead are great to dry, be placed in sachets, and hung as wardrobe fresheners.
Back to Ancient times: when a Roman girl married, she wore a Flammeum, an orangish - Flamma is the Latin word for flame - veil surmounted by a wreath made of marjoram and verbena flowers. Although with time, myrtle took their place, and again later orange blossoms.
In the Middle Ages, monks used to make marjoram oil for its curative properties. It warms and relaxes the neuro-muscular system. And, if massaged on the body, it fights insomnia, especially the one caused by fear and anxiety.
To make a small try-it-and-do-more-if-it-works-for-you bottle, you can:
Buy or harvest about 15 gr/0.5 oz of fresh marjoram - half the quantity if dried.
Pestle it in a marble mortar to help it release its healing oils.
Transfer it to a small jar and cover it with about 50 gr/1.8 oz (about four tablespoons) of extra virgin olive oil.
Let it rest one to three days in a dark place.
Drain the oil through a cheesecloth, squeezing the herbs to get every drop of essence.
Store it in a clean glass bottle or jar.

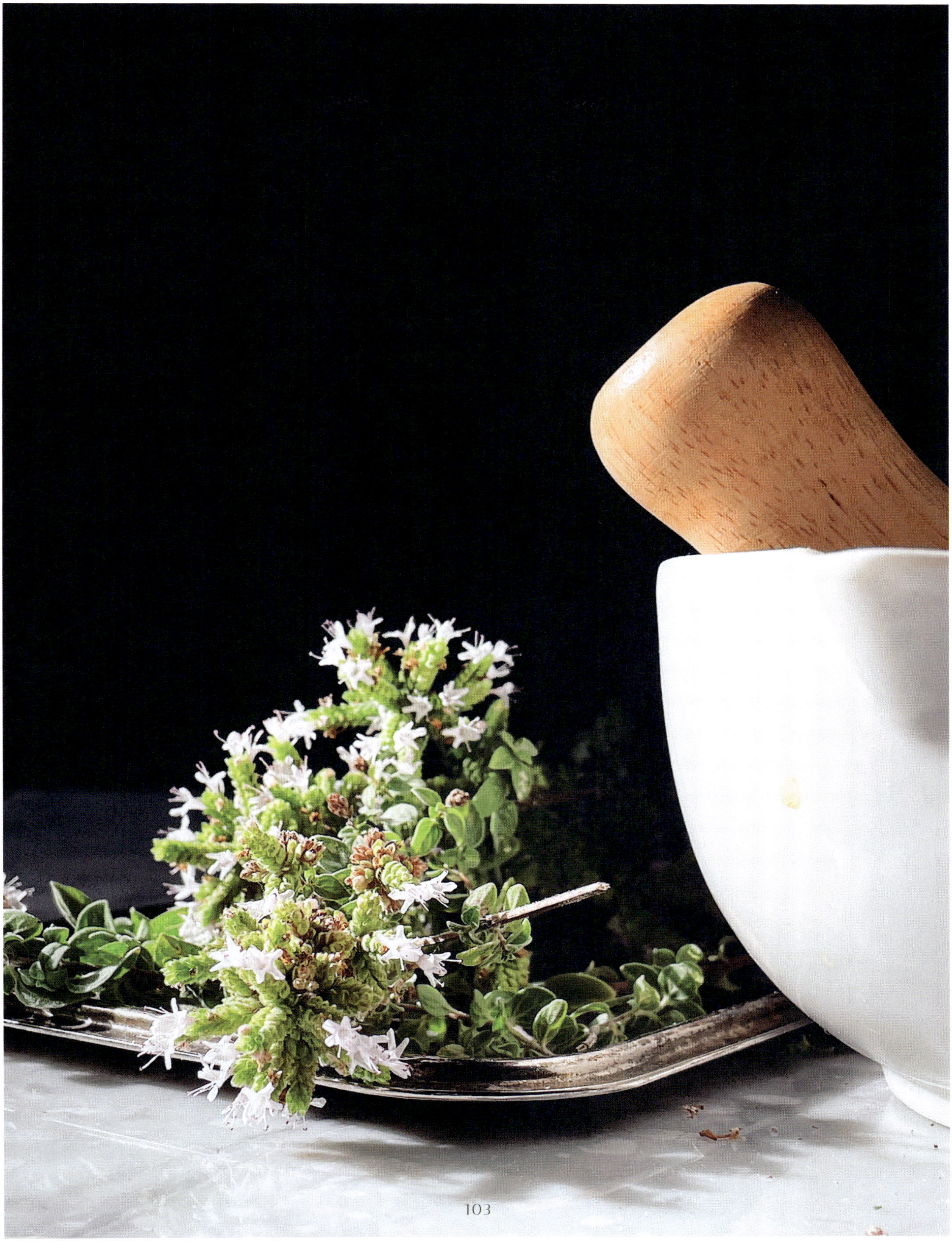

PASTA ALLA NORCINA

I mentioned earlier that when we want to break the diet, we Italians drive to Norcia. Sit at a rustic table with a boar head hanging next to us. And order a Tagliere Misto: a charcuterie board. Next, we will almost certainly be served a plate of Pasta Alla Norcina. Norcino is the pork-butcher that apparently, prepares his pasta with sausages and ricotta.

Ingredients for two:
160 gr (5.6 oz) of spaghetti or Tortiglioni pasta
100 gr (3.5 oz, about 1 sausage) of Italian sausage
2 tablespoons of ricotta cheese
1/4 white onion
1 garlic clove
1 tablespoon of extra virgin olive oil
salt
pepper
30 gr (1 oz) of black truffle - optional

Bring a big pot of salted water to a boil - about two liters (half a gallon) and one tablespoon of salt.
Peel and finely chop the onion. With the blade of a large knife, crush the garlic clove - no need to peel it.
In a medium pan, heat the olive oil, add the garlic and onion, and brown them - about five minutes over medium heat.
Meanwhile, peel the sausage and shred the meat with a fork.
Toss the pasta into the boiling water and cook it according to package directions.
Remove the garlic from the pan - discard it - and add the sausage. Brown it on medium heat and stir every now and then until a soft crust starts forming.
Collect about a quarter cup of the pasta water and keep it handy.
Add the ricotta to the sausage pan and pour in the pasta water. Stir energetically to amalgamate all flavors and create a soft, creamy coating around the meat.
Drain the pasta and add it to the pan - or return it to the pot and pour the condiment in. Mix thoroughly.
Sprinkle your pasta with abundant pepper and the shaved truffle if you wish.

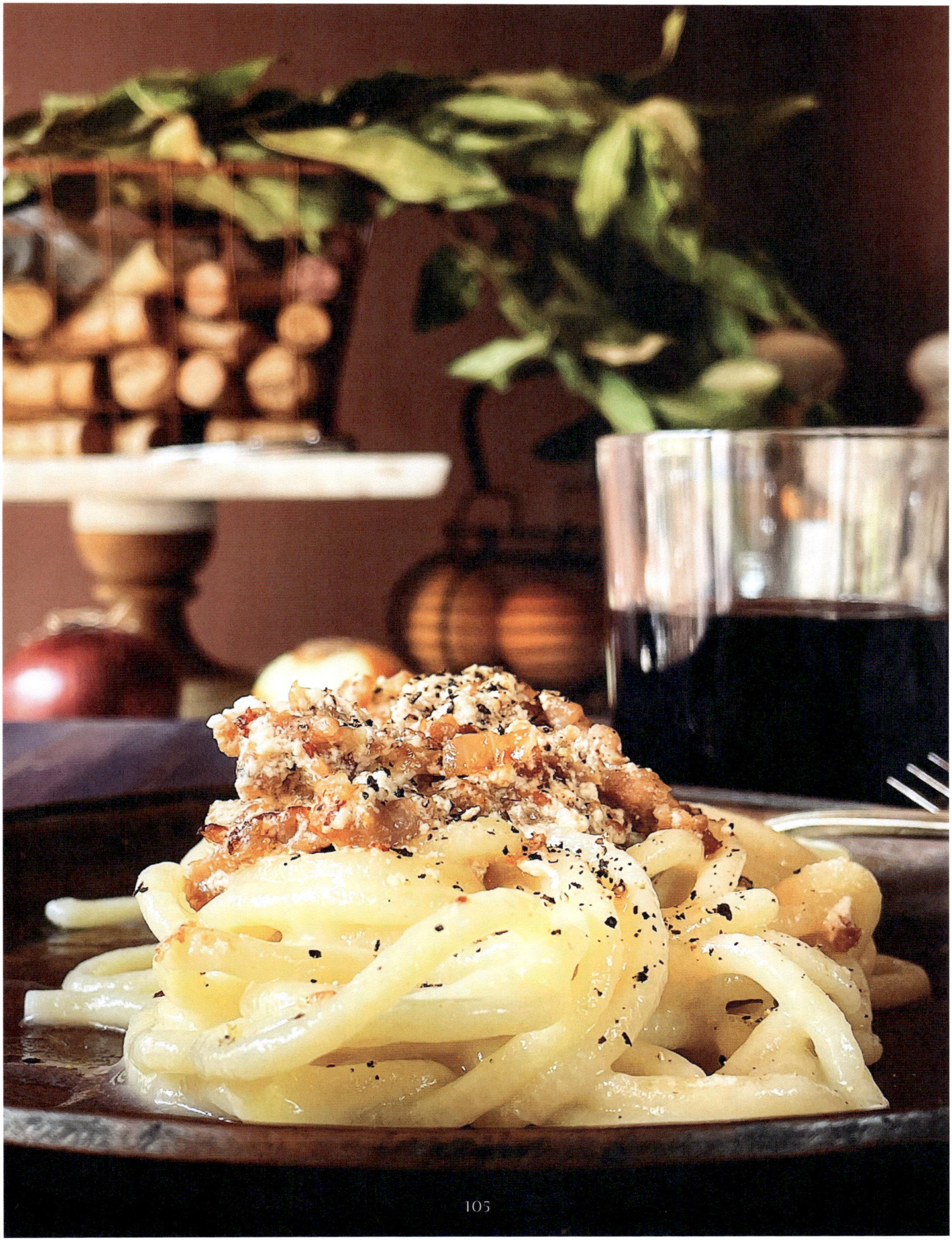

LENTICCHIE IN BIANCO

Please allow me to dedicate this traditional Norcia recipe, lentils "in bianco" (no tomato), to Santuccia, a witch from Norcia. She was burned at the stake in 1445.
All the people that had asked for her cures in the previous years or who had climbed the solitary mountain where she lived for a medicine or a remedy, decided, one day, to denounce her. They told the Inquisition that she had killed fifty children and chosen one of them to drink his blood, acquiring it from his ear. This after profaning a communication host. It had been given to her by a priest, poor thing, taken by his genitals and slung against a tree through a spell.
Although the law admitted the payment of four hundred Lire to redeem the sorcerer. Although Santuccia had half of the money. No one in town offered to lend her the rest. Not even those she had saved, cured, and taken care of.
Imagine if she could come back. What would she do to those people?

Ingredients for two:
150 gr (5.3 oz or 3/4 cup) of Norcia lentils
1 garlic clove
1/2 celery stalk
extra virgin olive oil
salt

Slice the celery stalk into small pieces.
Place the lentils in a medium pot, add enough cold water to cover them, add the garlic clove - peeled - and the celery.
Turn on the heat to high until the water boils, then reduce it enough to get a continuous simmering. Cook twenty to twenty-five minutes, add a teaspoon of salt - more or less upon your palate - and taste for readiness. If needed, add water, and cook until the lentils are tender but not squishy.
Once cooked, find, and discard the garlic clove, then let the lentils rest for ten minutes.
Serve them hot and sprinkled with a few drops of extra virgin olive oil.
If you want to make soup, simply keep the lentils more moisturized and don't let them dry completely.
Then toast four slices of rustic Italian bread, place them in two serving bowls, and cover them with the lentil soup.

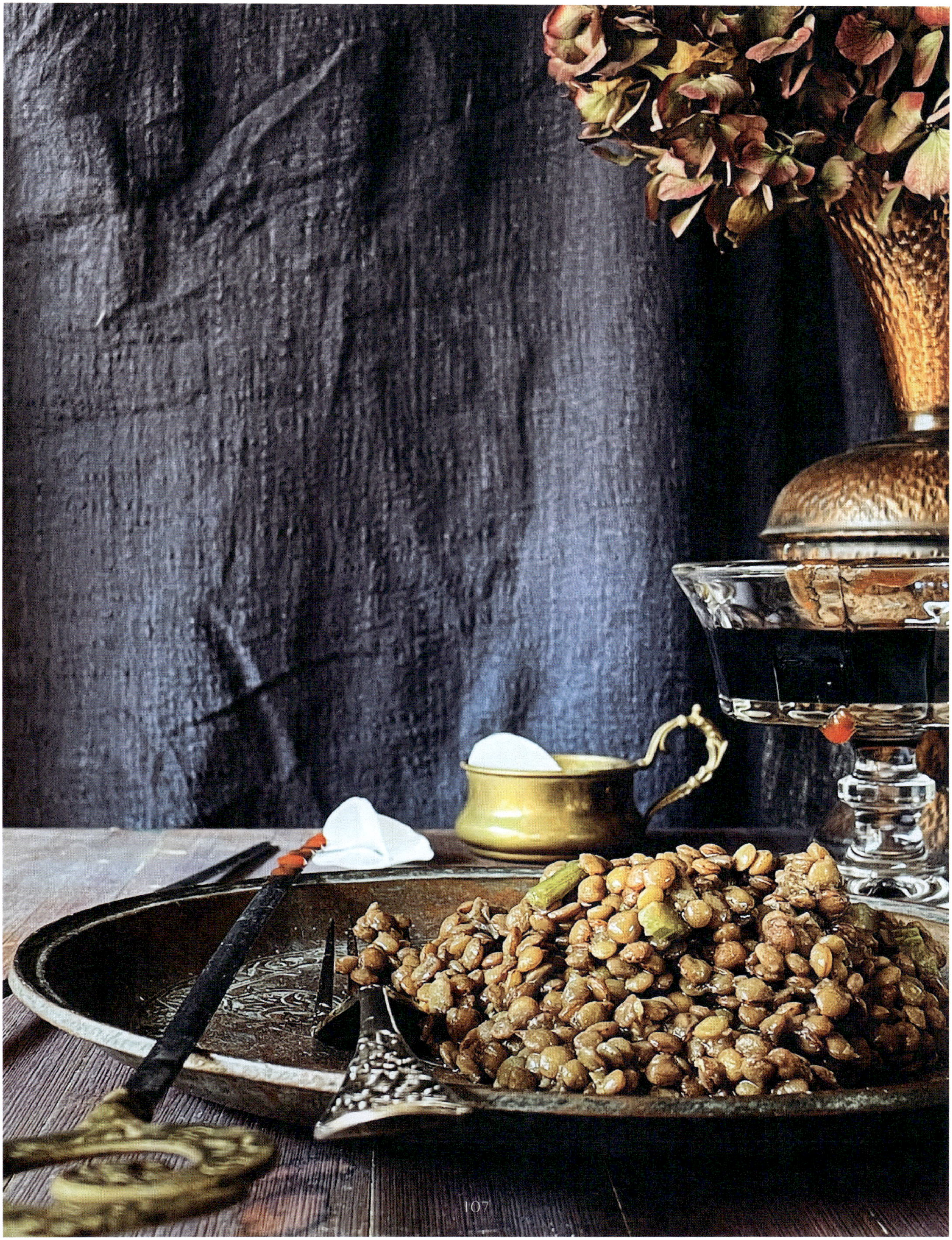

LU PIZZALLOCU

Lu Pizzallocu is a sweet bread that once was made for the shepherds of Castelluccio Di Norcia - a town near Norcia, on their way to Maremma. It is a tradition to eat it with Giuncata cheese.

Ingredients for two to four:
250 gr (8.8 oz or 1 + 1/2 cups + 2 tablespoons) of 00 flour
2 tablespoons of sugar + more for garnishing
50 ml (1.7 oz or 4 tablespoons) of cow milk + a few drops
1 egg
2 tablespoons of extra virgin olive oil
6 gr (0.2 oz or 1 teaspoon) of baking powder
the zest of 1/4 lemon
1 pinch of salt - 1/4 teaspoon
1 egg yolk

Place the flour in a mixing bowl (or mixer with the kneading hook on). Add the sugar, milk, olive oil, baking powder, egg, lemon zest, and salt. Mix until you get a consistent dough, one you can work and shape with your hands. If needed, add milk or olive oil - one tablespoon at a time.
Once you can form a ball, continue working it for about five minutes - two with the mixer.
Preheat the oven to 180°C/350 °F.
Shape the dough into a rustic loaf and place it on an oven sheet lined with parchment paper.
Beat the egg yolk with a few drops of milk and brush the surface of the loaf. Then dust the surface with about a tablespoon of sugar.
Bake forty minutes until you get a dark gold surface - insert a knife or skewer into the center; if it comes away clean, it's ready; if it has batter, the cake needs a few more minutes.
Enjoy hot or at room temperature.

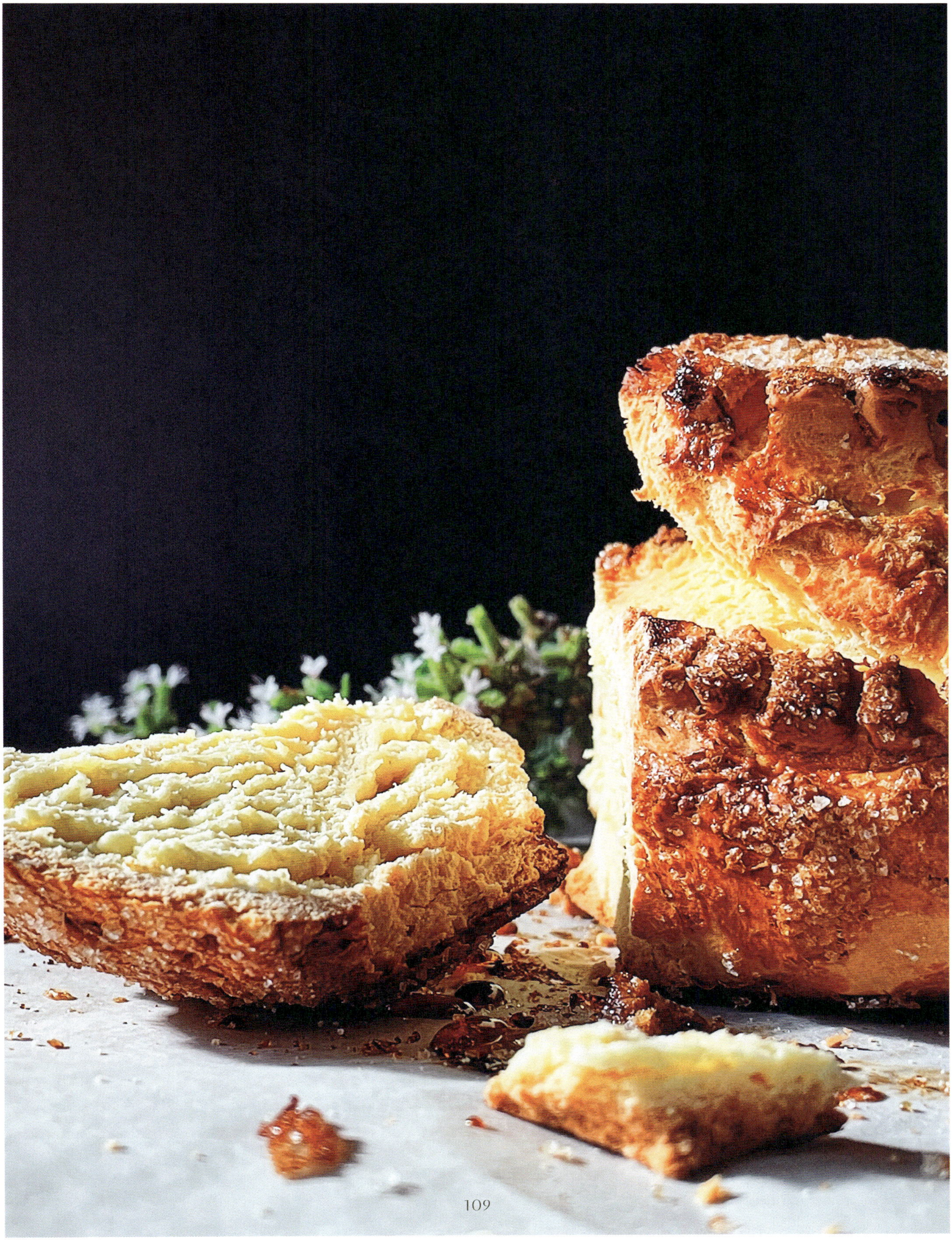

SCHEGGINO

Scheggino was enchanting. We arrived at the golden hour on a winter day, soon darkening. Christmas decorations were still on. It was like visiting a crib. Climbing the stairs meant encountering rocky walled doors sublimely decorated. Sometimes it was a plant, other times a string of lights. A vase with dried flowers or a Christmas tree. Ornaments were rare, always tiny. How does it feel to live in a place so beautiful it is the ornament itself?

It was also freezing. Of the near four hundred residents, the only people we saw were a man unloading the car with what looked like supplies for the cold weather and two kids playing soccer. Although I have no idea how they could, being every alley downhill. I guess childhood creates its own rules. But ribbons of smoke came out of the houses. Usually, when I visit little towns like this, I hear messy television noise. It annoys me quite a bit. It deprives the place of its allure. I imagine zombies, victims of commercials. Minds manipulated by terribly reported news. It's the opposite of when I see elderly people outside, on the porch. Chatting or sewing. Or reading! That, in my realty-denying mind, is appropriate to the place. I want to believe there's something left of a time when the Terza Media - more or less 8th grade in the United States and two years before GCSE in the United Kingdom - was enough to guarantee a vast culture of history, literature, poetry, Latin, and Greek*. When men and women dedicated themselves to activities much nobler than a reality show. The fact that prosperity brings decadence is pretty undigestible to me.

So Scheggino, with its silent aisles and smoking houses, happened to be the fertile ground I needed to fantasize about a town of culture. I imagined people nestled in their homes reading a historical treatise. Nonni reading Greek mythology to their nephews. Someone knitting. Someone playing cards. After all, it was still the holiday season.

To furtherly nourish my imagination, I reminded myself that Scheggino is the place that celebrates women. How avant-guard is that for a tiny village perched in the middle of the Umbrian mountains?

Every year, on July 23, Scheggino stages a historical reenactment where women are the protagonists.

It was 1522, and a league of Umbrian cities was rebelling against Spoleto. Scheggino was the city's loyal sentinel and refused to cooperate. The commandants of the rebellious decided to attack when the town would've been most vulnerable, during the reaping,

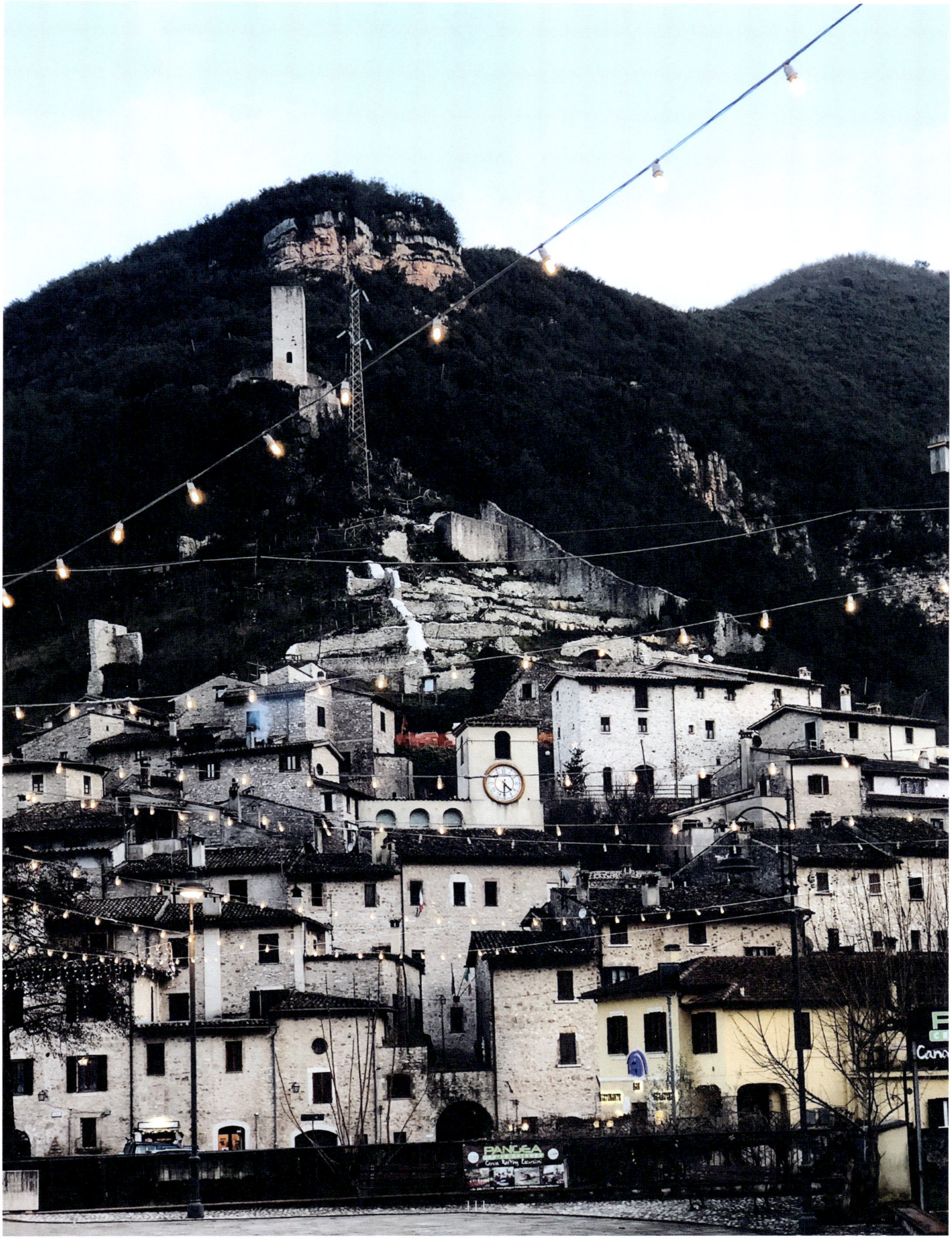
PANGEA

when the men would be in the mountains, and the women, the elderly, and the children would be alone and helpless.

For three days, the fortress was under attack. For three days, the helpless battled. The senior citizens and the children threw rocks against the soldiers. The women heated and poured oil from the walls. Again, and again.

When they sensed that the soldiers were exhausted - and they had probably run out of oil - the ladies armed themselves with whatever pointed or sturdy object they could find and took to the main piazza. With rocks, sticks, wooden pieces, and cookware, they battled. Hostesses, housewives, seamstresses, and cooks scared away the troops. And won the battle!

A few months after the "Festa Delle Donne", Scheggino is ready to celebrate once again. With Faoni: huge bonfires lit on the night of December 9. The once pagan celebration in honor of the reveler fauns is now a welcoming and guiding-through-light ritual devoted to the angels that flew the Sacred House from Nazareth to Ancona (a city in the Marche region). Schegginesi spend the evening around the fires, tasting the new wine and other local delights. When the town bell rings, they run home. It is time to eat the "Pizza Della Fortuna", a focaccia cooked under the ashes. One of them will find the coin hidden in the tasty dough and be blessed for the coming year!

Another convivial moment for Schegginesi happens on January 6, the Befana Day in the rest of Italy, the Pasquarella - first Easter - for Scheggino and other central Italy towns. At around two in the afternoon, a group of youngsters moves from house to house. They play and sing the Pasquarella. Folk songs pleading for food - "if you give us a sausage, it won't stick to our teeth", which makes more sense in Italian as it is a rhyme - and wishing religious blessings. Once a cart towed by a donkey accompanied them, nowadays a mini tractor. Clearly, the pleaded homeowners open their doors and pantries. They donate sweets, bread, salami, bottles of wine, and more.

I may be a dreamer, I may live out of reality. But if these traditions have lived to date, it must mean there are people of culture behind them. People that still care. Who spend their winter days behind those rocky walls, planning the celebrations, teaching the limericks to the kids, sewing costumes, and drying the wood. This is what I decide to believe. This is what I'm telling you and what I'll recount to whoever will want to listen. Precious counterculture.

*Ruca Ricolfi, an Italian sociologist, in his La Società Signorile Di Massa, asserts that, nowadays, it takes an average of eight more years of studies to reach the same cultural level of a Terza Media diplomat in 1962.

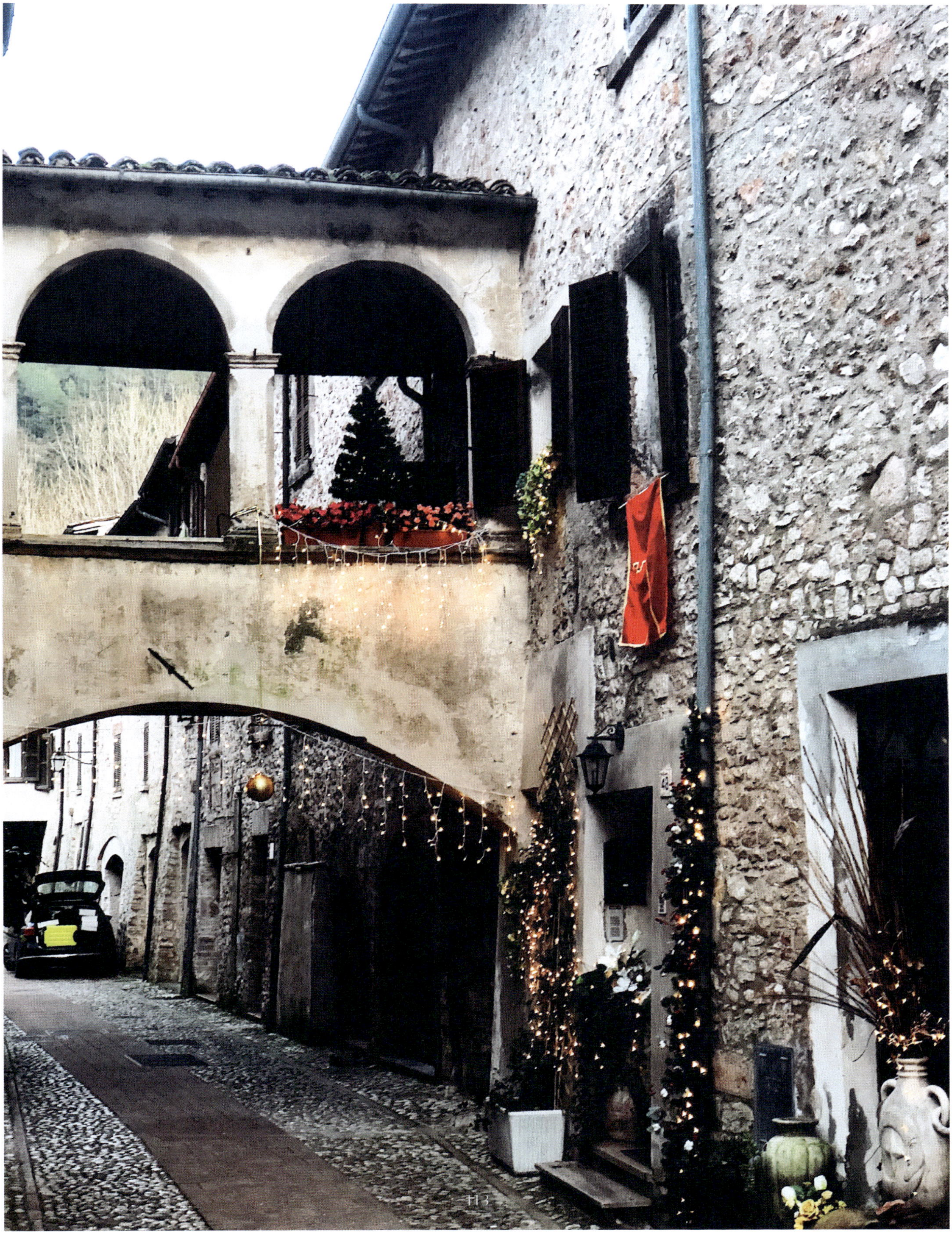

LUMACHINE ALLA SCHEGGINESE

More snails! Not actual snails, but I sense there's something going on between Umbri and the little creatures. In this case, it is the pasta shape, you can find it called both Lumachine and Pipe Rigate. Or you can use other short pasta shapes.
As in other cases of traditional dishes, the first and second courses are cooked together. This way, proteins flavor the sauce - trout and tomato for this recipe - for the pasta and are served afterward. The trout fillets remind us that the river Nera crosses the downhill area of Scheggiino. And a rain of truffle flakes that we are in Umbria.

Ingredients for two
200 gr (7 oz) of Lumachine or Pipe Rigate pasta
400 gr (14 oz) of trout fillets - about 1
1/4 onion
2 tablespoons of extra virgin olive oil
250 gr (8.8 oz or 1 cup) of tomato paste (Passata)
40 gr (1.4 oz) of black truffle
salt
black pepper

Peel and finely chop the onion.
In a large pan, heat the olive oil and sautè the onion over medium heat until translucent - about five minutes.
Add the trout fillets and cook them, medium heat, for five minutes - skin down for the first couple of minutes, then flip them on the other side.
Flip once more for the skin to be down, add the tomato Passata, a quarter cup of water, a pinch of salt, and a few grinds of pepper, cover, and cook at low heat for about fifteen minutes.
Meanwhile, shave the truffles as finely as possible - use a truffle or cheese shaver.
Remove the fish fillets and set them aside on a serving plate - they'll be the second course.
Add the truffle flakes to the sauce, mix delicately and turn off the heat.
Cook pasta according to the package directions. Drain it and season it with the tomato sauce.
Serve and enjoy both courses hot!

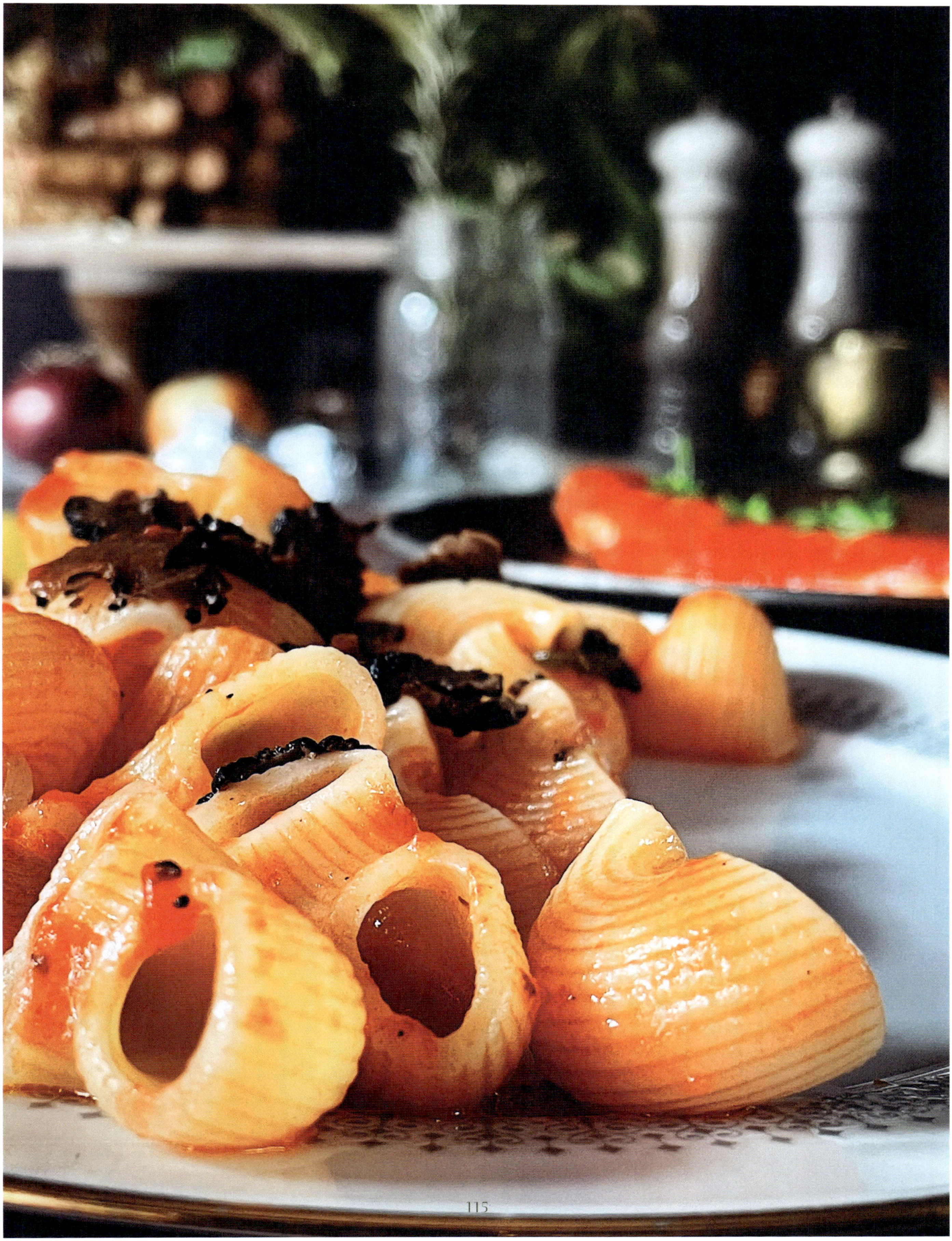

UOVO LENTO AL TARTUFO

It was a cold, rainy, and windy day. But I didn't care a bit. It was almost midnight, and my husband and I were dry, warm, and happy. We were sharing a bottle of Sagrantino with the chef of the restaurant in Torgiano and a couple from Rome we had befriended the night before - exchanging opinions on the plates we had ordered. It was one of those moments when you become mates in a matter of minutes. There's a parallelism you can't quite define between you and the people in front of you. The chef was a wine lover and melancholic painter. The woman reminded me of one of my best adolescence friends: chatty, Northern Rome accent and attitude, and extrovert. And her partner was my hero. An artist with a clear mission: bring back the art of mosaics.

I firmly believe - and people with way more credentials than me do, too - that it is around the table that these magical encounters happen. Food, when cooked with love and passion, is like a potion that opens your heart to strangers. Wine helps, of course. But there's something in the air, a golden powder dusted on your words to make them fly, swirl, and bring the true you to the ears of others. And back, their answer, their idea, their opinion. More gold to enrich the moment.

That night, we had ordered Uovo Lento Al Tartufo, scrambled at the perfect point, and covered with flakes and flakes of black truffle.

Ingredients for each serving:
2 eggs
30 gr (1 oz) of black truffle
1/2 garlic clove
extra virgin olive oil
salt

Heat a couple of teaspoons of olive oil in a medium pan.
Meanwhile, crush the garlic clove with the blade of a large knife - no need to peel it. Add it to the pan and brown it, medium heat for about five minutes.
Flake the truffle with a truffle or cheese shaver.
Remove the garlic, turn off the heat and let the temperature decrease a bit. Add the truffle flakes but keep some for garnishing. Let the remaining heat sauté the truffle and then remove it with the help of a spatula or spoon. Return the pan to medium/low heat.
Break the eggs into the pan, sprinkle them with a pinch of salt, wait until the bottom starts whitening, then scramble them. Add the toasted truffle flakes, and mix. It should take seconds for the eggs to be ready, cooked but still creamy.
Transfer them to a serving plate and top them with the raw flakes you kept aside.
Serve hot with toasted bread for a glorious Scarpetta.

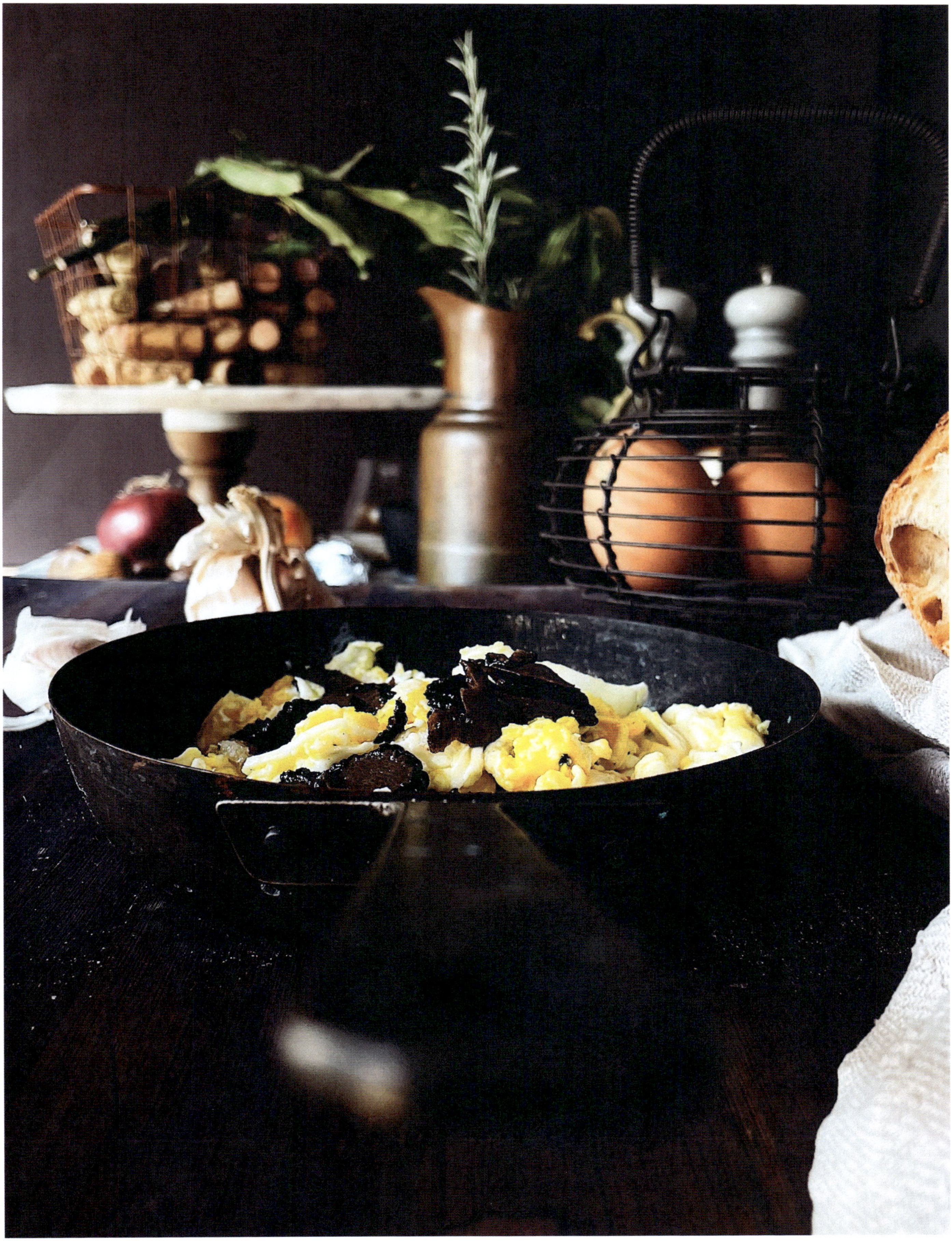

CHRISTMAS

As mentioned earlier, on our last trip to Umbria, we stayed in Torgiano, in an ancient residence. Upon our arrival, before the check-in, we were offered tea and cookies. We were set on a wooden, quilted with arabesque motifs, couch. In a living room developed around a giant chimney. There was a piano, a wooden, scratched-to-the-right-amount coffee table, and Umbrian landscapes hanging on the walls, next to a Caravaggio-style fruit basket. But please don't misunderstand me. Nothing was expensive nor showy. It was classic. And not the magazine-styled, nothing-out-of-place classic. It was more like being hosted by a family. A wealthy family with ancient habits catapulted to the present. A family you could fantasize of: they must've been hunters, winemakers, hard workers, and a bit isolated. A tad conservative, very traditionalist.

Even the Christmas decorations were that kind of classic. Those placed around by a mother with many kids and little time. Who has inherited some beautiful handmade ornaments and bought, not bothering too much at the quality, materials, or whatever modern obsession, the other decorations.

It was real. Hence cozy.

The umpteenth confirmation to my not-so-original suspects: Christmas needs a soul more than anything else. It needs traditions, lightness at heart, and letting a bit of nature in.

I'm trying to fit in. I'm trying to rediscover my family and country's traditions. But also introducing some that are mine, unique. The result of contaminations from my other country of origin. From my journeys around the world, and my sense of aesthetic. But most of all, I'm trying to be there. While I craft, while I put on the decorations, and afterward, for the efforts to be worth it.

In the past years, I've tried many new things. I once - or twice -, on the night between the 12th and the 13th of December, put out of the window a cup of coffee and some cornflower. For Santa Lucia and her donkey, bearers of Christmas gifts before the Santa Claus colonization.

I once robbed a log from my father's chimney - we can't light it in Rome, but he lives a little outside. And I decorated it and placed it in my chimney.

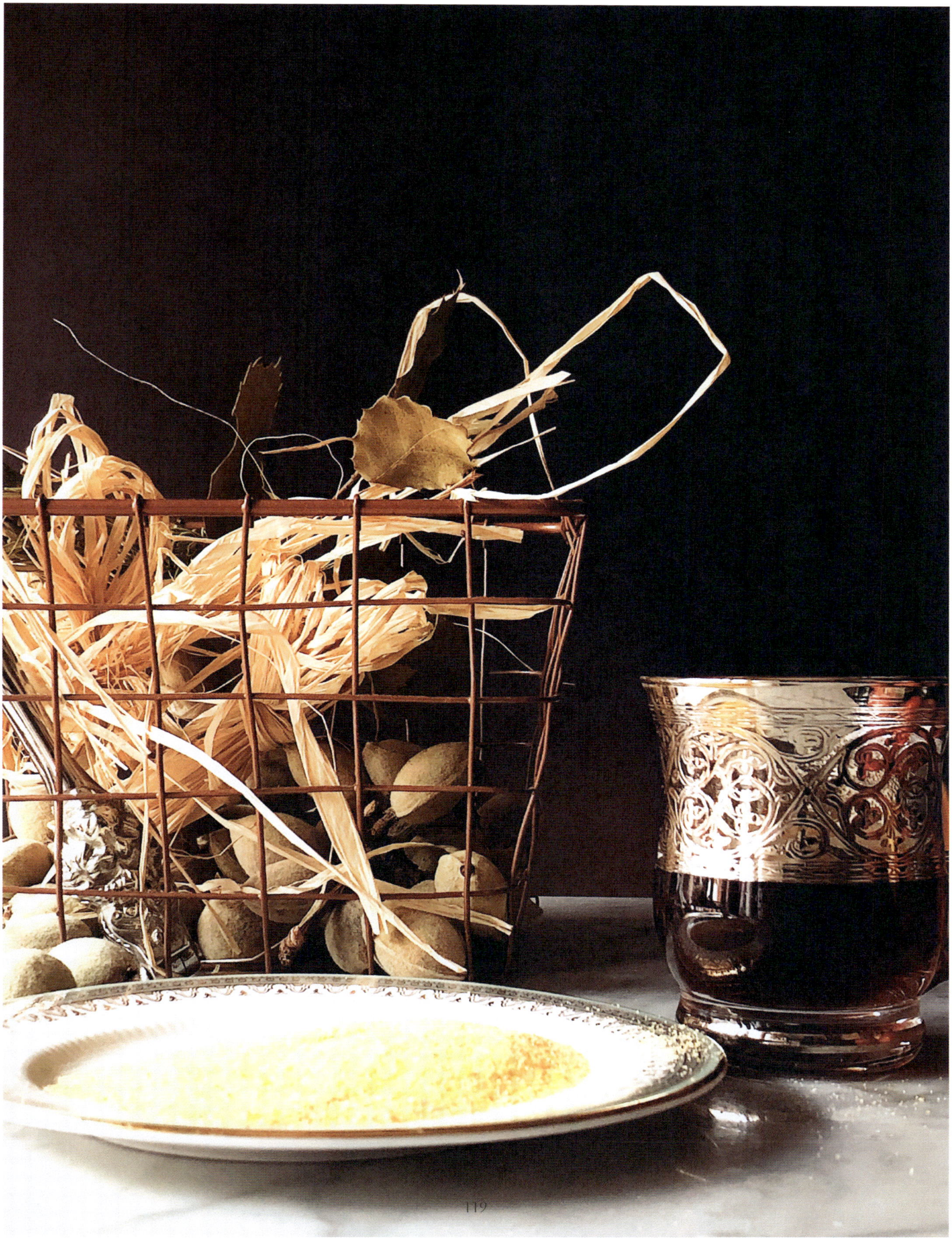

To honor the ancient rite of lighting it on the 24th of December and again for twelve nights until the epiphany.

I more than once dried orange slices to decorate the Christmas table, the mantel, or the Christmas tree.

I added pomegranates to a Christmas cake stand already full of nuts and dried red bulbs, as a folkloristic symbol of good luck.

Last year, I also found a lady that makes Hallacas, the elaborate, delicious Venezuelan dish for Christmas. I boiled the stuffed cornmeal dough wrapped in plantain leaves. Opened a great bottle of Sagrantino. Set on the table and shared with my husband a piece of my childhood.

That same year, I wrapped the gifts in fabric - roughly dyed during a rainy Sunday and waited impatiently for a sunny day to properly dry. I wanted to emulate the Japanese Furoshiki: fabric squares to wrap gifts or to carry things around.

Even if I wanted, I could never be an integralist. I am half and half, I love traveling more than anything, and I welcome contaminations like a drunk welcomes yet another glass of vodka. But I like to think of myself as someone who respects identities. Who values traditions and their precious contributions to making life a wonderful journey. I can't think of a global world where we are all the same. It would bore me to death. I am because you are.

In our differences, we find ourselves; thanks to our differences, the time spent together is enriching. If I could, I'd spend the year celebrating everyone's festivities, tasting their traditional food, learning rituals and beliefs. How extraordinary would a life be if it could absorb all that wisdom, all that love, all that fun. Looking back to look forward.

Could it be that what we humans were destined for was a huge banquet, a never-ending symposium, a constant exchange of points of view and feelings? Socialization, so they call it.

Evolution, I add.

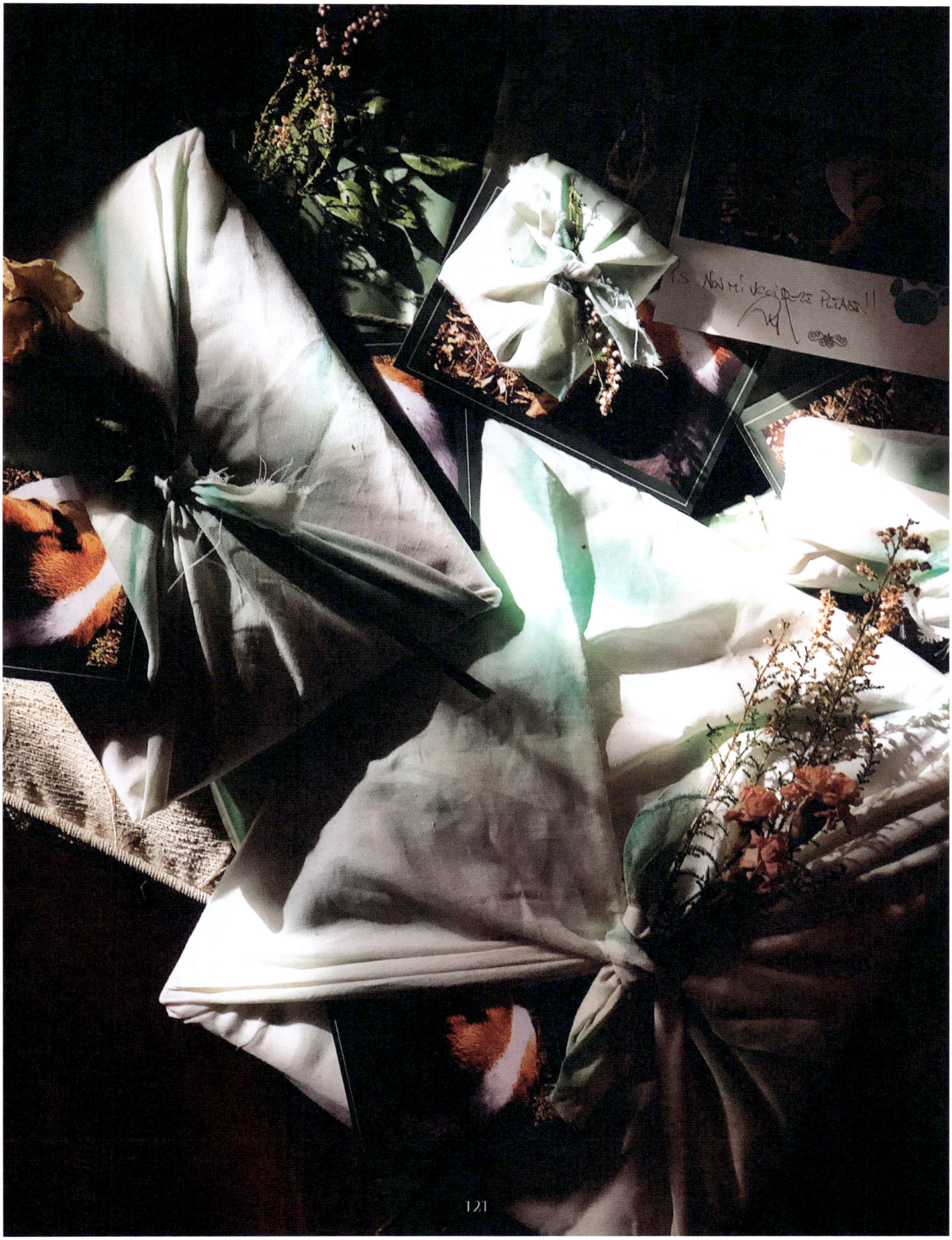

STELLE DI NATALE

There's a scene I see every Christmas since I was just a little girl: people on the streets of Italy carrying a Stella di Natale, the Christmas star. Which is not an ornament but a plant.
The Poinsettia, I've learned, is a holiday symbol in many other places of the western world. But I hadn't researched the reason why, the legends, and the characteristics of this plant. Let's do it together!
Euphorbia Pulcherrima is original of Mexico. The Aztecs used the bracts to extract a purple dye for clothes and cosmetics, while the sap was worked into a medicine to treat fevers.
The Christmas Star was introduced to Europe in the early 1900s. Accompanied, of course, by a legend. During a Christmas Eve mass, a girl was crying because she had nothing to offer to baby Jesus. An angel appeared by her side and reassured her nothing would be more precious than the flowers she could pick outside the church. The girl ran out and came back to add her humble gift to the very showy, very beautiful, and very precious gifts from richer devotees. In not a remarkably Christian mood, people began murmuring and deriding the girl's bouquet, but only until the wildflowers became giant, magnificent, and scarlet flowers. Only, they weren't flowers. The big pointed and velvety petals we see are the plant's bracts - modified leaves. The actual flowers are the small, yellow clusters in the center of the star-arranged leaves.
Let's go back to the streets of Italy and the ribboned vases my compatriots carry around. You can be sure they are directed to a family gathering or that they were invited by friends. Because Stelle Di Natale are most often given - not purchased for oneself - to thank for something. Tradition has gifted this plant a strong symbology. The star shape represents Bethlehem's star, while the red color represents Jesus's blood. In floriography, the language of flowers, Poinsettia expresses love for the neighbor. In France, indeed, it is called Étoile d'amour, the star of love. The falling and returning leaves symbolize the renovation of a new year. And the bracts that intensify in color as Christmas approaches, the return of solar fire, the promise of abundance, and the return of the good season.
It will be with other eyes and another state of mind, I believe, that both you and I will look at these plants. Their purchase will be an intentional, heartfelt act.

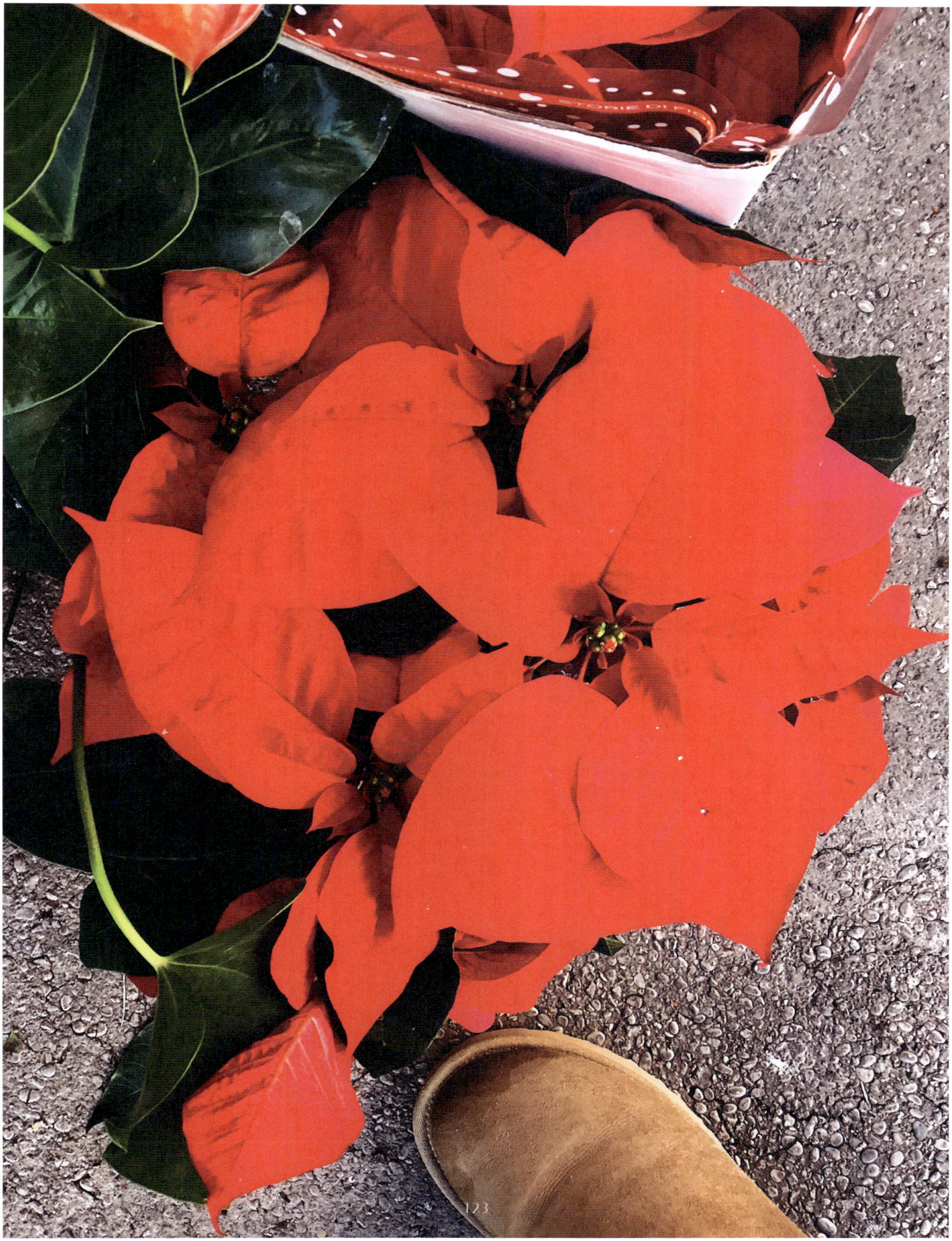

BOILED CHESNUTS

Let's end with a little, sweet fall cooking.
My whole life I have roasted chestnuts in the fireplace when in the mountains and in the oven at home. Inside the dedicated pan with holes or simply scattered on an oven sheet. But last year, I learned a new way: boiling them with aromatics.
It's a new thing, well, an ancient recipe here in Italy, but something fancy for us.
You can try them for, let's say, a movie night!

Ingredients:
one to two dozen chestnuts
two bay leaves
one tablespoon of fennel seeds
salt

New tip: I recently learned that soaking the chestnuts for about an hour in a bowl of water rehydrates them, and you get a more tender fruit.
With a small knife, engrave the rounded side of each chestnut horizontally. Try to carve the shell and not the fruit.
Place the chestnuts in a pot and pour water to cover them completely. Toss in the bay leaves and the fennel seeds.
Bring to a boil, add a pinch of salt, lower the heat, and simmer for thirty to forty minutes. Timing depends on quality and dimensions. It could take you up to sixty minutes. Fetch one, peel it and taste it for readiness.
Once done, drain them and let them cool for about twenty minutes.
Finally, peel them and devour them!

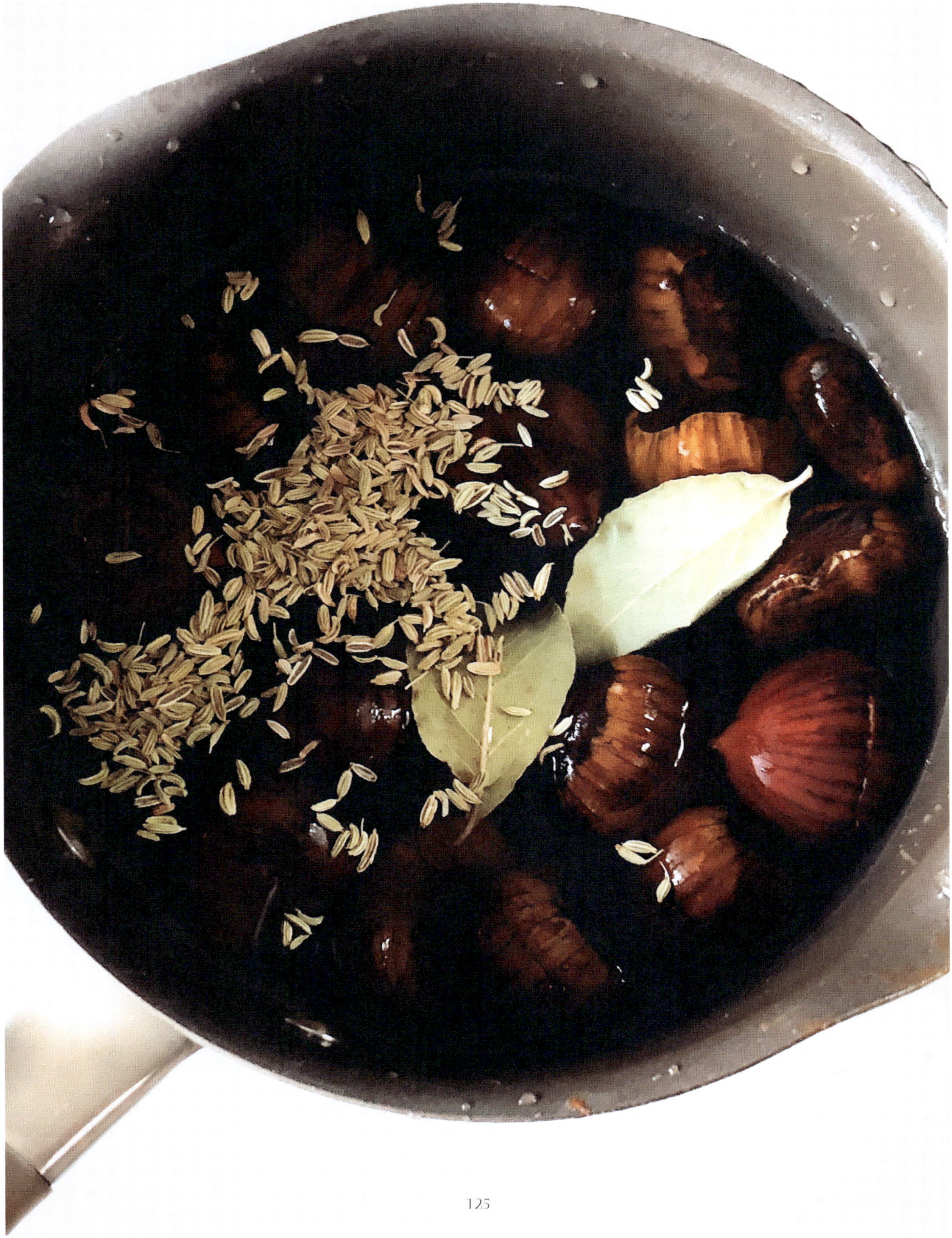

GRAPE JUICE OVERNIGHT OATMEAL

This is a recipe that is not exactly a recipe: it's too easy.
But it's a delicious idea for the lovers of oatmeal breakfasts, but haters of cooking when still half-asleep. Overnight oatmeal is your ally. I've experimented with many ways to make it, but my favorite is with fruit juice or, better, pulp!
Grapes are perfect because they're so sweet you don't need to add anything else.
Maybe a pinch or two of cinnamon.

Ingredients for each serving:
1/4 cup of oatmeal
2 cups of grapes

Juice the grapes with the juicer, an extractor, or my way: I blend them just enough to juice and filter them through a fine sieve. I leave them dripping for a while, although I could accelerate things by pressing with a spoon. But I'm lazy.
Place the oatmeal in a jar, pour in the grape juice, and refrigerate overnight. Voilà, breakfast is waiting for you.

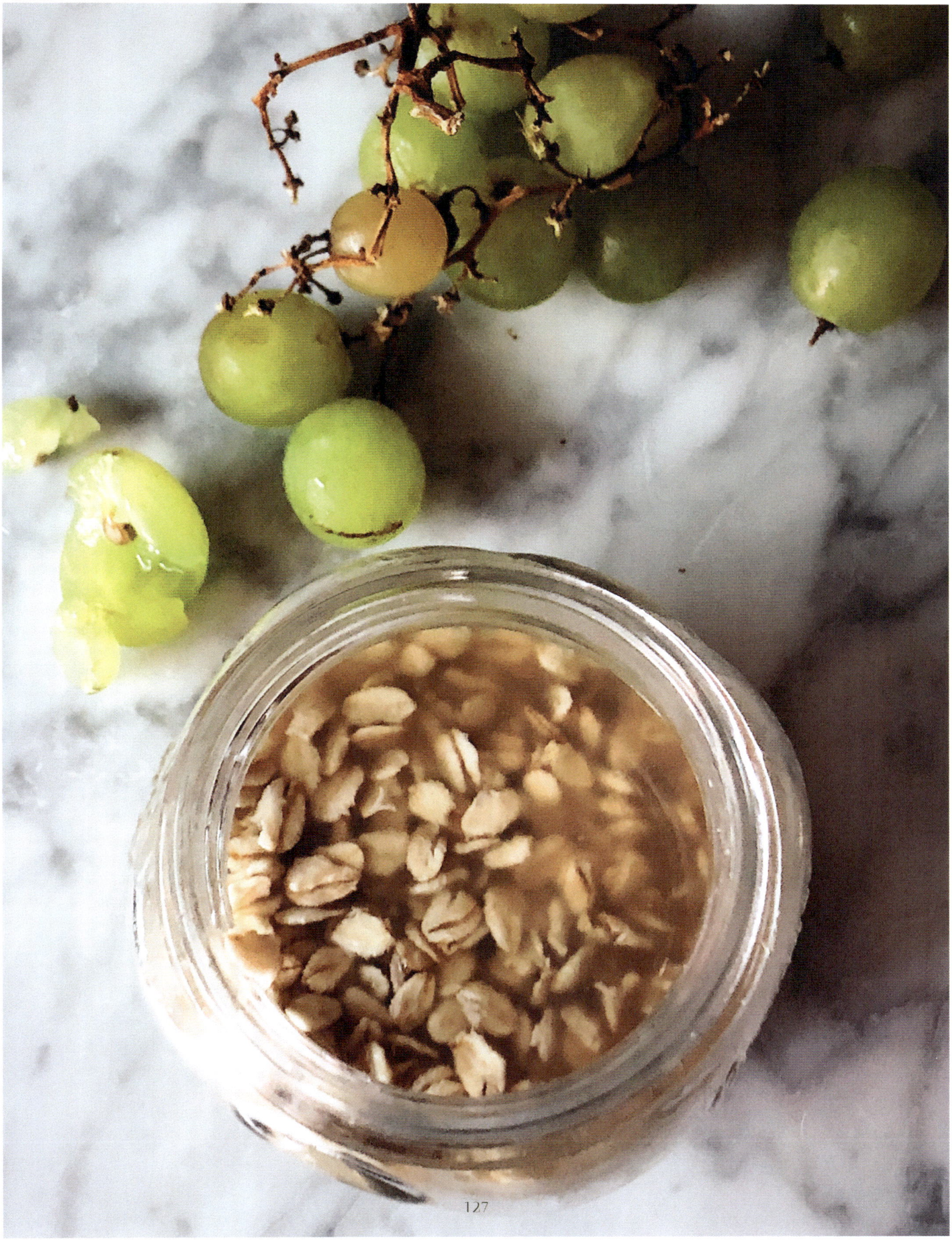

NONNA CLARA'S MACKEREL PASTA

Recently, we discovered another common culinary passion: the strong and pungent taste of mackerel fillets in olive oil.
This is how she makes a delicious pasta dish. As always, her cuisine is all about combining many aromatics. Plus, she rarely skips an anchovy or two.

Ingredients for two:
200 gr (7 oz) of long or short pasta
140 gr (5 oz) of mackerel fillets in olive oil - net weight
1 garlic clove
1/2 onion or scallion
1 tablespoon of salt-cured capers
1 tomato - salad or heirloom
3 anchovies
1 tablespoon of dry oregano
1 tablespoon of fresh basil
1 tablespoon of fresh parsley
extra virgin olive oil
salt

Place the capers in a small cup and cover them with water.
Peel and crush the garlic clove with the blade of a large knife. Peel and finely chop the onion.
Heat one tablespoon of olive oil in a large skillet, medium/low heat. Brown the garlic clove for about five minutes and discard it.
Add the onion and sauté for five minutes or until golden.
Bring a big pot of salted water to a boil - about two liters (half a gallon) and one tablespoon of salt.
Meanwhile, drain and squeeze the capers and finely trite them. And dice the tomato.
Add the capers, the tomato, a couple pinches of salt, and the dry oregano to the skillet. Cook, always medium/low heat, for approximately ten minutes.
Toss the pasta into the boiling water and set the timer as per the package directions.
Add the anchovies to the skillet - move the tomato pieces to make space -, smash them with a wooden spoon, and mix them with the tomato. Cook a minute or two. Add the mackerel fillets and shred them slightly with a fork or wooden spoon. Finely chop the parsley and add it too.
Mix and cook five minutes more.
Drain the pasta and add it to the skillet.
Add the basil leaves, mix well, and serve hot.

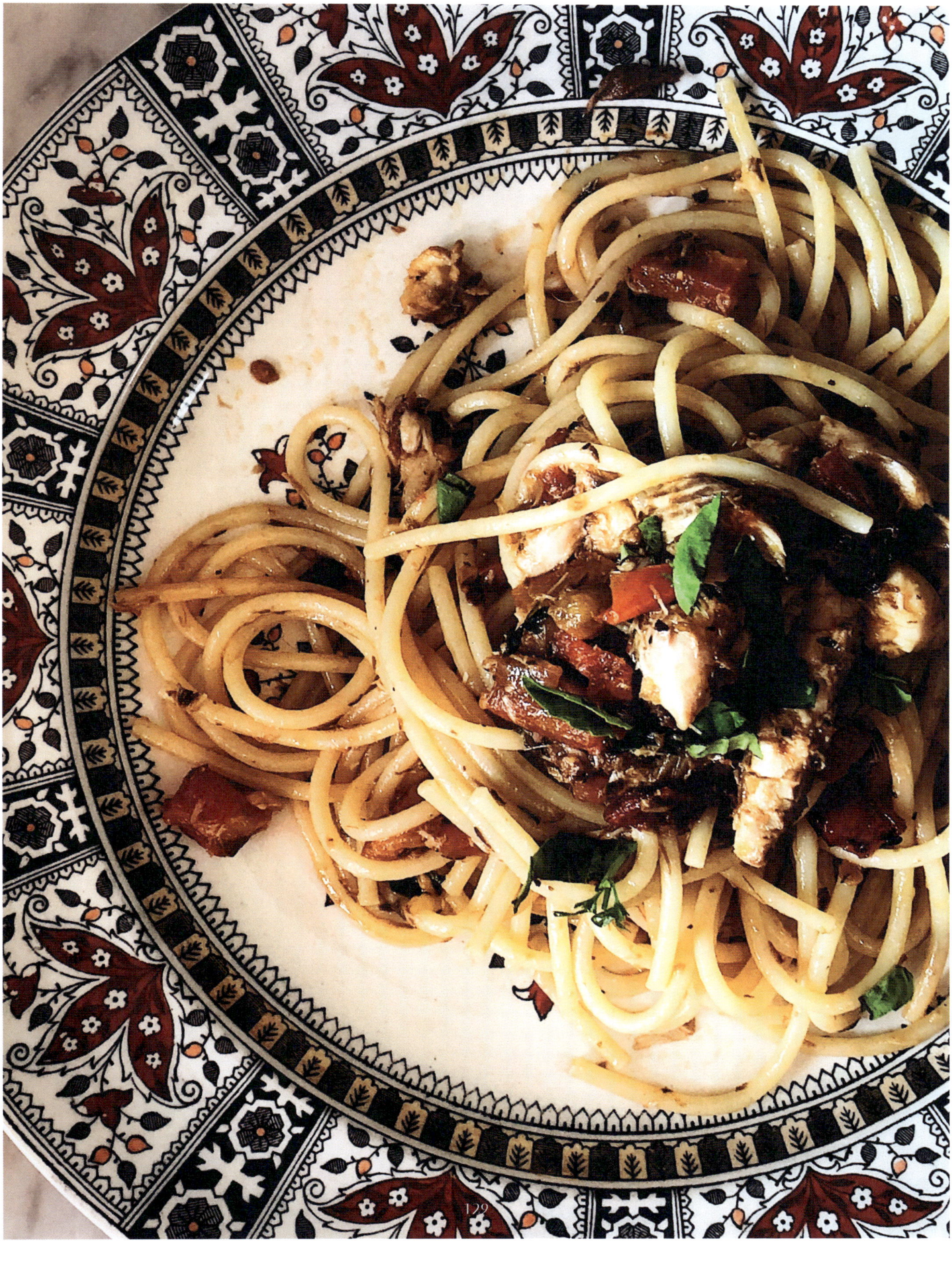

BROCCOLI CREAM AND GRILLED SWORDFISH PASTA

This is a recipe created one day, putting together leftovers and the telling of my husband of a delicious pasta he ate at his Tuesday lunch with the friends that work in his same neighborhood.

Ingredients for two:
200 gr (7 oz) of spaghetti
4 broccoli florets (including stems)
1 medium swordfish fillet
1/2 garlic clove
nutmeg
extra virgin olive oil
salt

Clean the broccoli florets and shave a little of the stems to remove external filaments.
Sprinkle them with a pinch of salt and steam them until fork tender (ten to fifteen minutes).
Meanwhile, bring a big pot of salted water to a boil - about two liters (half a gallon) and one tablespoon of salt.
Heat a medium pan for about five minutes. Pour in a tablespoon of olive oil and grill the fish fillet, four minutes on one side and three to four on the other.
Remove the skin from the filet and dice the meat.
When the broccoli florets are cooked, transfer them to the food processor or a bowl if you are going to use a hand blender. I left out a few tiny buds for garnishing.
Add a couple to four grinds of nutmeg, a teaspoon of olive oil, the garlic clove peeled and thinly sliced, and a pinch of salt. Pulse or blend until creamy and well amalgamated.
Cook the pasta in the boiling water al dente (one minute less than packaging directions).
Drain the pasta but keep half a cup of the cooking water. Add the pasta to the pan, add the broccoli cream and a few tablespoons of the cooking water, mix well over high heat. If necessary, add the remaining water, but don't overdo it: you want the pasta covered in cream but no liquids.
Add the swordfish cubes, mix, and serve hot!

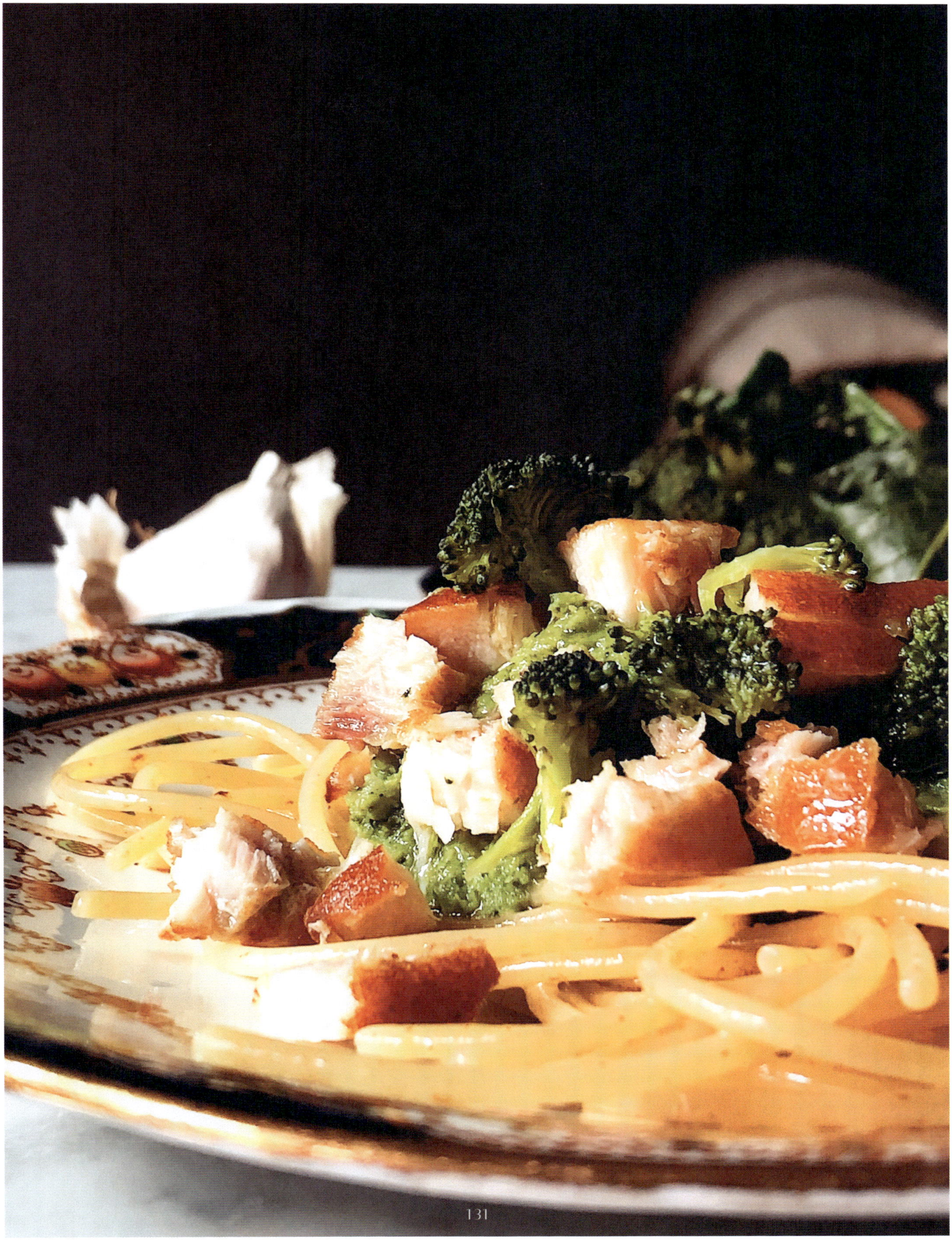

On the next issue

Next time we meet, we will ride horses, walk on the beach, and visit the Tuscan Maremma. Get ready to meet brigands, eat at a Jewish table, and fish in a lagoon!

See you soon

Claudia

Claudia
THE AUTHOR

My name is Claudia, I'm half Italian and half Venezuelan.

I live in beautiful, romantic, charming Rome. I love to cook, travel and dance - alone, in my living room. I collect, and wear all the time, hats, and I hunt the world for vintage china and cutlery.

My mission is to show the world that Italy is so much more than pasta and mandolino, although... don't you dare take away pasta from me!

You can be part of my Gourmet Project by:
• visiting the blog: www.gourmetproject.net for more recipes and Italian stories;
• subscribing to the Italian Colors newsletter for weekly bites of Italian food and culture;
• subscribing to SIMPOSIO or getting the other issues of the mag: all seasonal but evergreen content!

a presto! - see you soon!

Anna
THE EDITOR

My name is Annamaria and I am of Irish and German descent living in the USA. (Nashville, IN)

I love to cook, write, and play music. Not only am I an avid cook, I am also a firm believer that my table should look as beautiful as the meal I place upon it! I'm currently working on a series of children's books, "The Adventures of Princess Penelope".

Sláinte Irish Gaelic – to your health as well

NOTES

Printed in Poland
by Amazon Fulfillment
Poland Sp. z o.o., Wrocław
22 December 2022

761a3b23-ee80-4ff7-acbb-4177c6b51161R01